ABSTINENCE

Members of Overeaters
Anonymous Share Their
Experience, Strength,
and Hope

ABSTINENCE

Members of Overeaters Anonymous Share Their Experience, Strength, and Hope

OVEREATERS ANONYMOUS.

ISBN 0-9609898-7-0
Library of Congress Catalog Card No.: 94-67576

Overeaters Anonymous, Inc.
World Service Office
6075 Zenith Court
Rio Rancho, NM 87124
Mail Address: P.O. Box 44020
Rio Rancho, NM 87174-4020
(505) 891-2664
www.overeatersanonymous.org

Printed in the United States of America

NOTE: In 1995, the World Service Business Conference delegates adopted the following change in OA's tools of recovery: "To remove abstinence as a tool and replace it with a "plan of eating," leaving abstinence as our primary purpose as outlined in the OA preamble: 'Our primary purpose is to abstain from compulsive overeating and carry the message of recovery to those who still suffer.'"

PREFACE

This book is a collection of stories and essays on the topic of abstinence. All were written by members of the Overeaters Anonymous Fellowship and were published between 1989 and 1993 in *Lifeline*, OA's monthly magazine. The opinions expressed are those of the individual writers and do not represent OA as a whole. Their words are not intended to give a definitive or ideological answer to our questions about abstinence; rather, they represent to us many different examples of experience, strength, and hope.

Whether you are a longtimer with many years of abstinence, a member struggling with recovery or relapse, or a newcomer to whom the subject of abstinence may still be a mystery, may you find encouragement, help, and direction within these pages.

CONTENTS

One – The Meaning of Abstinence

Two – Practical Ways to Achieve Abstinence

Three – The Search for Abstinence

Four – Abstinence – A Priority

Five – Abstinence and the Tools

Six – Abstinent Living

Seven – How Abstinence Changes With Time and Experience

Eight – What Abstinence Has Taught Me

One

THE MEANING OF ABSTINENCE

1962 — ABSTINENCE ENTERS OA

Eager for information about our early years, members frequently ask me: "How did the idea of abstinence come into OA? Was it always the way it is today? How did it start?"

Looking back, the years from 1960 -1962 were exciting for us. We were so impulsive, so eager to see our tiny Fellowship grow and establish a firm foundation. By 1962 we were united about the wording of our twelve steps and twelve traditions. In other areas, however, we all had different ideas on how to achieve our common goals.

Consider food intake, for example. Before 1960 most of us had grown up counting calories. We had been taught that as long as we kept within our calorie count, we could eat all the barely caloric foods we wanted between meals.

Our problem was that while many of us had lost weight, even more were nibbling their way back to obesity. Others were sticking with their diets but crunching all day on the low-cal foods. Many just stayed fat, insisting they were only eating allowable foods between meals. Something crucial was missing. What was it? The twelve steps worked for our Alcoholics Anonymous (AA) friends; what were we doing wrong?

During those years I was going to AA meetings every week. Although I'm not an alcoholic, my understanding of the steps and traditions was so limited I believed I could learn more by attending AA.

In early 1962, one powerful AA meeting changed my way of thinking about eating. All through that meeting the speakers emphasized "abstinence" from alcohol. During the two years I'd had contact with AA, I had never heard sobriety referred to in that manner. It was a revelation!

Sitting in the back of that meeting, I thought to myself: "That's what's wrong with all of us in OA. We're not abstaining from food at any time of the day. We have to close our mouths from the end of one meal to the beginning of the next. Sometime during the day, we must 'abstain' from eating; otherwise we're feeding our compulsion."

Excitedly I brought my new approach back to OA. Some thought it was a breakthrough; others scoffed.

By spring of 1962 we counted nineteen OA groups, most of them in California. The OA office was in my little dining room, and I was the unofficial, unpaid national secretary. We had already had our first informal meeting of the Los Angeles area groups; now we agreed it was time to have a real conference of all OA groups.

TOGETHER WE CAN CLIMB THOSE TWELVE STEPS TO RECOVERY, ABSTAINING FROM COMPULSIVE OVEREATING ONE DAY AT A TIME!

Therefore, in May 1962 I sent out an *Overeaters Anonymous Bulletin* (forerunner of today's *Lifeline*) to all OA groups. It introduced secretaries and group starters to one another and mentioned the proposed Conference.

Then on page three of that first *Bulletin* came the announcement that would both unify and upset us for decades:

"Out of our regular visits to AA meetings and talks with our friends in Alcoholics Anonymous, we here in the Los Angeles area have discovered a concept that has revolutionized our way of thinking about our compulsive overeating.

"That concept is 'abstinence'.

"Abstinence means simply three *moderate* meals a day with absolutely nothing in between. It means also no 'meals' while we're preparing a meal and no 'meals' while we're cleaning up the kitchen afterward. In other words, total abstinence from compulsive eating!

"If for medical reasons our doctor has ordered more than three meals a day, then of course we would plan accordingly and know that anything outside that plan would be breaking abstinence. Of course, black coffee, tea, water, and noncaloric beverages of any kind are the exception to between-meal nibbling.

"Just as the alcoholic must totally abstain from alcohol to remain sober, so we have found we must totally abstain from compulsive eating to maintain our own kind of sobriety. We call those who have achieved this kind of sobriety 'abstainers'.

"There are no 'musts' to any part of the OA program . . . indeed our twelve-step program is only a suggested plan for recovery. Therefore, we aren't saying that abstinence is a 'must'. We're only passing on to you what we have learned from our own experience . . . that with 'abstinence' from compulsive eating we have at last found the true meaning of sobriety for the compulsive overeater."

In 1962 this was a brand-new idea for us. Since the word *abstain* means "to stay away from," it seemed clear that to be abstinent in OA meant to stay away from compulsive overeating. How to do this? Since we must eat, the most logical method would be to eat only at mealtimes: That meant three moderate meals a day, more if health needs required them, and absolutely nothing in between.

Unfortunately, over time abstinence took on a new meaning, a corruption of the original. Instead of implying "to stay away from," it came to suggest the eating plan itself.

"What's your abstinence?" one member would ask another. What the person really meant was, "What's your eating plan?" With this confusion, it's no wonder the word *abstinence* has come to mean different things to different people.

Will the time come when we all understand that the concept of abstinence is the same for everyone . . . to stay away from compulsive overeating? Can we recognize that it is the eating plan which may be different from one person to another, perhaps different for an individual at various times in his or her life?

In 1962 my unexpected insight was difficult to grasp, even harder to put into practice. Today it is no easier, but we *can* meet the challenge. Together we can climb those twelve steps to recovery, abstaining from compulsive overeating one day at a time!

A MANY-SIDED TREASURE

Abstinence is freedom — freedom to say, "No, thank you" to that dessert because my desires have been changed. I used to eat because I couldn't say no, and I couldn't stop. Abstinence frees me to choose healthy foods, friends, and thoughts.

Abstinence is inner peace and clarity of mind to see that cravings, confusion, emotional binges, and excess pounds are all I'm giving up.

Abstinence is a gift from God. It's the number one action in my life so that God can be in the center. Abstinence frees me to hear God speak through others and through readings.

Abstinence is strength and power. God's power has become available because of my powerlessness. The longer I am abstinent the stronger new habits become and the faster old destructive fantasies fade from my mind. It establishes a new way of life.

> ABSTINENCE IS STRENGTH AND POWER. GOD'S POWER HAS BECOME AVAILABLE BECAUSE OF MY POWERLESSNESS.

Tampa, Florida

A STATE OF GRACE

Abstinence is a state of grace by which I am balanced physically, emotionally, and spiritually. It's about food, but it's much more. It's a way of living that incorporates the principles of the twelve steps and gives meaning to my life.

I've developed a routine that places God first in my life, and this has led to my success with abstinence. When I awake in the morning, I first say hello to my Higher Power then mentally take the first three steps. I admit I am powerless over food and that, try as I might, I can't control my life. I remind myself that H.P. is restoring sanity to me. The final part of my morning ritual begins with the Third-Step Prayer from the Big Book. I conclude it by saying: "If it be Thy will, today I will follow my food plan and avoid binge foods. I will do something nice for someone today, and I will be happy. Thy will not mine be done."

This surrender to H.P. and my daily commitment to abstinence have added an emotional balance to my life. Without the negative feelings caused by bingeing on sugar, I am able to sail through the day on calm waters. If old feelings of irritability,

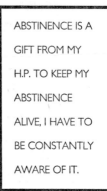

ABSTINENCE IS A GIFT FROM MY H.P. TO KEEP MY ABSTINENCE ALIVE, I HAVE TO BE CONSTANTLY AWARE OF IT.

discontentment, and restlessness pop up or when food thoughts surface, I repeat program phrases to myself over and over. "Easy does it." "Just for today." Usually this does the trick, but if my distraction stays with me I write about what I'm feeling. Then I share what I have written with a sponsor and follow through with any other steps that need to be taken.

Abstinence has added a spiritual dimension to my life. My mind and heart thank H.P. throughout the day with affirmations such as, "Thank you for the gift of abstinence."

Abstinence is a gift from my H.P. To keep my abstinence alive, I have to be constantly aware of it. I have to work my program continuously. I study the Big Book and OA materials, and I live in an "attitude of gratitude" for the miracle of Overeaters Anonymous.

Louisiana

A WAY OF LIFE

"What is Abstinence?"[1] caught my eye in *Lifeline*. When I read the article I discovered that it wasn't a summary of OA abstinence wisdom — it was an invitation to submit my own definition. So I suggested to the other members of my group that we get together and share our ideas. It turned out to be a wonderful experience for all of us.

---

[1] A request for submissions for our special abstinence issue.

We discovered that abstinence is about living, choosing, accepting, admitting, affirming, turning it over, and trusting God to take care of the results.

Abstinence is enjoying God's food the way it's meant to be enjoyed. It's eating healthy food with a prayerful, surrendered attitude. We allow ourselves to be satisfied with the amount of food we need, instead of the amount we want or think we need.

Living life abstinently is participating fully instead of self-isolation. It's being free of shame, mortification, and self-condemnation. It's replacing negative self-talk with positive affirmations, many times a day, in many ways. It's being at peace within ourselves, knowing we have done our best. We find that there are no good guys or bad guys. We don't have to agree with or please everybody. We don't have to get involved in debates over

ABSTINENCE IS ENJOYING GOD'S FOOD THE WAY IT'S MEANT TO BE ENJOYED.

who's right and who's wrong. We can speak our minds and feel at peace. We don't have to control the other person's reactions to what we say or do.

In abstinence we can learn to feel good about ourselves. We can love and accept ourselves just as we are. Our freedom from compulsive overeating rests in the hands of each individual's Higher Power. We live in a daily miracle. We trust our Higher Power to take care of us, even if we get hungry.

We learn that each of us is a special and unique part of God's picture. We begin to treat ourselves in a different way. Our illusions drop away and we get in touch with reality. We learn to feel the feelings, face the pain, and deal with it. We discover an inner strength that tells us that we are worthwhile in spite of what others have told us in the past.

We begin to realize that it is a choice between life and death. Abstinence means choosing life and compulsive overeating leads to death.

Honesty becomes our way of life. We can tell the truth and trust our perceptions. Our wonderful qualities become apparent to us as we accept them and cherish them.

We exercise our right to be here, our right to be respected, and our right to be listened to and understood. We no longer allow ourselves to be victimized by others.

This miracle of abstinence is a message of recovery. It allows us to extend our hearts and hands to those who still suffer. When we are abstinent, we can be truly present for other people who are in pain.

Ukiah, California

A CALL FOR DEFINITION

In 1988 the World Service Business Conference passed a policy that stated, in part, "Abstinence in Overeaters Anonymous is the action of refraining from compulsive overeating." This was the same statement I heard when I started in OA twelve years ago.

I have always accepted this as a complete description of abstinence. It is short, precise, and leaves no room for doubt. But we are still having "food fights" within the Fellowship. I believe there are two reasons for this. First, it is unclear to many that there is a difference between abstinence and a food plan. Second, and most importantly, we have never defined what compulsive overeating is.

The food plan issue is easy to address. I have concluded that even though abstinence is the same — or should be the same — for everybody, food plans vary widely. At one end of the spectrum are those who don't need one in order to maintain abstinence, while those at the other end must have a carefully timed and measured plan. Neither approach is right or wrong to me. Abstinence is our goal, and whatever one must do to achieve it is acceptable. The variations in our individual food plans may frighten some members, but we can each hold on to the constant of abstinence as serene reassurance.

Defining compulsive overeating is much more difficult. Perhaps because AA didn't feel it necessary to define alcoholism, OA hasn't yet defined compulsive overeating; but the boundaries concerning alcohol are much clearer than food. We know what an alcoholic drink is; we don't always know what a compulsive bite is. Likewise, we know — even by legal statute — what "drunk" is, but we don't know with certainty if someone has binged.

I'm not going to attempt to define compulsive overeating at this time. My reason for writing this is to generate interest in defining it. I believe a definition would greatly help our Fellowship. We could more easily inform the public and the professional community about OA by accurately describing the illness we have. Within OA, we would retain more members as they come to understand exactly what their disease entails and accept there are no absolutes for food plans, for there are many facets of compulsive overeating.

> I HAVE CONCLUDED THAT EVEN THOUGH ABSTINENCE IS THE SAME — OR SHOULD BE THE SAME — FOR EVERYBODY, FOOD PLANS VARY WIDELY.

As important an issue as abstinence is, I'm convinced our program should remain rooted in the twelve steps, practiced within the protective framework of the twelve traditions. Is abstinence the most important aspect of our program? My answer is decide for yourself, keeping within the spiritual nature of Overeaters Anonymous and with the help of a loving God.

Overland Park, Kansas

IT'S SIMPLE AND IT WORKS

My abstinence is three meals a day. I defined it that way on purpose the first day I came to OA because I didn't want abstinence to seem like a diet and because I wanted it to be something I'd stick to. In the first few weeks of abstinence I found eating just three meals a day was much more difficult than I thought it would be. I was hungry and thought about food a lot of the time. After about a month I got used to it and found that I really looked forward to those three meals, and I enjoyed not having to think about eating in between. My abstinence became, as I've heard other OAs describe it, three meals a day with *life* in between.

Now that I've had a few more months in the program, I've begun to really appreciate having a simple three-meals-a-day abstinence. My eating isn't always perfect, nor is it always guilt-free, but the fact remains that no matter what I may have eaten for my meal, the meal has an end, and I don't eat again until the next one. This represents a major change from my eating pre-OA. Then, if I'd broken a diet even a little bit, it was an excuse for binge eating. Now my imperfect three-meals-a-day abstinence means I can finish whatever it was I had for dinner and say that's all till breakfast.

> MY EATING ISN'T ALWAYS PERFECT, NOR IS IT ALWAYS GUILT-FREE, BUT THE FACT REMAINS THAT NO MATTER WHAT I MAY HAVE EATEN FOR MY MEAL, THE MEAL HAS AN END, AND I DON'T EAT AGAIN UNTIL THE NEXT ONE.

I think relapsing or breaking my abstinence would be easy for me to recognize because I feel certain that if I started eating a fourth meal I would continue until I had an undeniable, full-blown binge on my hands. I acknowledge having had a "slip" if I have a bite of something and think better of it, or if I eat a larger meal than I need to and feel guilty about it.

Weight gain is another issue entirely. I take weight gain as a sign that I need to work the program more consistently. Usually when I examine what's going on within me I discover that not only have I been eating more and more of less and less healthy foods, I've also been skipping meetings and not reading, writing, or using the telephone.

All I can do in response is footwork. My bottom-line, no-frills abstinence is a major part of that footwork. It keeps me in the program and reminds me at least three times a day that I am powerless over food. It's kept me coming back one day at a time, and I'm twenty-two pounds lighter than I was when I walked in.

Los Angeles, California

A PROGRAM OF MANY COLORS

Abstinence: It can baffle, direct, control me. It tells me if I'm a "good OA" or in relapse. It gives me the means to proudly (or is it humbly?) say, "I've been abstinent for x number of days, weeks, months, years." Only by its grace can I be blessed to help another compulsive overeater.

For me there are two kinds of abstinence: the *tool* I used to help me get through the first nine steps; and the *gift* I received that stays with me on a daily basis if I keep in good spiritual condition.

Early in my OA program I needed to learn discipline when it comes to food, and so I used abstinence as a tool. I found it paradoxical to surrender to a new form of control. I had admitted I was powerless over food, and my life and eating were unmanageable. By using the tools, OA gave me a new way to control my food — I learned to call my sponsor before difficult meals like potlucks or dining out and to eat a normal amount of food at each meal. I began to eat not to lose weight, but in a way I could eat every day for the rest of my life. Even if I was not yet rational when it came to food, the amount of food I ate was. No more deprivation. No more waiting for the end of a diet when I could eat lots again. This was forever, one day at a time.

> EARLY IN MY OA PROGRAM I NEEDED TO LEARN DISCIPLINE WHEN IT COMES TO FOOD, AND SO I USED ABSTINENCE AS A TOOL

During this three-year period, I sometimes put my dependence on gum or diet soda to get from one meal to the next, and I often white-knuckled it. But there were also periods, sometimes a day, sometimes as long as a week, when I got a foretaste of the freedom from compulsive overeating that is promised in step nine. I knew my abstinence wasn't going to be a struggle forever, but until I finished the "recovering" steps, I had to be willing to fight my desire to overeat with every tool in OA, including my strict, controlled form of abstinence.

After almost ten years working our twelve-step program of recovery, I have experienced a different phenomenon — freedom from compulsive overeating. This is something different than three weighed-and-measured meals.

This is *freedom*. What I eat and when I eat are no longer central to my program — I no longer work on abstinence. It's not a tool I pick up in the morning and cut my way through life with. It's a peaceful sanity in relationship to food and eating. No more scales. No more fear of loss of control. Instead a trust in Higher Power and steps ten, eleven, and twelve keep me from indulging my old need to eat to cope with life.

I've had four slips (eating too much and feeling guilty about it) in ten years. After each slip I've needed to surrender again to a disciplined way of eating by weighing and measuring for a couple of days to get me back into sane quantities, freeing me to return to my "fit spiritual condition."

I do have some rules for myself. I stay away from certain foods because I have no good reason to eat them, and they've caused me trouble in the past. But if they're served to me I ask my Higher Power to help me decide sanely.

Abstinence is a tool and a gift. I've found it helpful to be patient and understanding with myself and others when we need to humbly use this tool, and grateful when I or others receive this precious gift.

South Africa

FREEDOM OF CHOICE

Nearly nine years ago, at my first OA meeting, I was introduced to the concept of abstinence. It took the form of enthusiastic applause from members at the mention of any length of abstinence — from day one to umpteen years. At the break, some members explained to me that abstinence was refraining from eating compulsively. That didn't mean much to me, but I kept coming back because those people had something I wanted; I just wasn't sure what it was.

During the next four months I learned many things about our common disease, not the least of which was that one symptom is perfectionism. This is one of my most devastating character defects. As a perfectionist, I set unbearably difficult standards for myself, and just as I am about to attain them, I redefine an even more difficult standard. I learned early on, and am still convinced, that the pursuit of perfection is a wasteful, stressful preoccupation. Many members offered me some valuable insight into perfectionism, and gave excellent examples of the toll it had taken in their lives and the steps they had taken to make progress in this area.

I STRONGLY BELIEVE THAT IF FOOD WERE MY SOLE PROBLEM, I WOULD NOT BE A COMPULSIVE OVEREATER.

But for many OA members there was apparently one exception to the process of becoming less of a perfectionist, and that was in regard to abstinence. I continued to hear more about abstinence at every OA meeting, but it seemed not everyone defined abstinence the same way. I heard about "perfect back-to-back" abstinence. This term received the loudest and longest applause. I also heard about "gray sheet" abstinence, "sloppy" abstinence, "human" abstinence, "moderate meal" abstinence, and abstinence qualified by a host of other adjectives. In those days there often was little if any distinction between *abstinence* and *diet*. Most troubling to me was the unspoken notion that one was worthy in the eyes of OA only if one's abstinence was "perfect." I began to see people dropping out when they broke their abstinence or if they couldn't achieve the "perfect back-to-back" variety.

The longer I'm in OA the more convinced I am that there are many paths that one can successfully travel to attain the spiritual awakening mentioned in the twelfth step. For me, this also holds true for abstinence. At the 1988 World Service Business Conference, a statement on abstinence was adopted that read, in part, "According to the dictionary, abstinence means 'to refrain from'. In Overeaters Anonymous, abstinence means to refrain from compulsive eating. . . ." This was not new to me as this was the concept I'd first heard in OA. I think nearly everyone in the program agrees that to be abstinent means that you don't eat compulsively. Where there is disagreement is in the many differing views of what compulsive eating entails. I haven't seen a definition of compulsive eating, nor do I recall any attempt by OA as a whole to address this issue.

To me, compulsive eating (or overeating) is eating to feed my disease — not my body's nutritional needs. Therefore I am abstinent when I eat to feed my body and not my disease. This concept has become my ideal of abstinence. It is a goal I can never achieve perfectly, nor do I attempt to do so. I don't imagine there is a person alive who eats strictly for nourishment at all times. To be physically abstinent I only have to follow the food plan I choose for myself each day as best as I am able.

> OUR RESPONSIBILITY PLEDGE SAYS, "ALWAYS TO EXTEND THE HAND AND HEART OF OA TO ALL WHO SHARE MY COMPULSION; FOR THIS I AM RESPONSIBLE."

I strongly believe that if food were my sole problem, I would not be a compulsive overeater. Why I turned to food and compulsive eating — that is the basis of my disease. Bingeing, obesity, and eating in secret are but physical manifestations of my disease, which I have come to realize is emotional and spiritual.

Emotionally, I found that my reactions to my feelings — not the feelings themselves — are important components of my disease. Everyone has feelings — that's part of being human. But my reactions to my feelings were usually childish, negative, and self-destructive, and resulted in overeating. Working this program aids my emotional recovery by showing me how to deal with my feelings in a positive, adult, self-loving way. Practicing abstinence is one way to do this.

Spiritually, I believe my compulsive overeating resulted from my building barriers to keep my Higher Power out of my life. Abstinence removes these barriers and puts me in conscious contact with my Higher Power. Perfect emotional and spiritual abstinence is not attainable, just as perfect physical abstinence is not attainable.

In OA, we are free to follow any eating plan we choose: if we need a strict, weighed and measured diet, we can have it; if we need to avoid only one specific food, that's what we do; if we need to change our whole approach because of changes in our health or any other aspect of our lives, we make that change. No one in OA disputes another's individual approach to emotional recovery, and certainly there is unquestioned tolerance regarding the choice of a Higher Power. Why, then, is there often encroachment on an individual's approach to physical recovery?

A slogan I heard at my first meeting was "progress, not perfection." I see this as applying to food as to every other aspect of the OA program. The more we as a Fellowship take such an approach, the more people will recover. I'm sad to say that I've known some members who gave up on OA and themselves because they couldn't live up to someone else's concept of abstinence. Our responsibility pledge says, "Always to extend the hand and heart of OA to all who share my compulsion; for this I am responsible." It doesn't say, to all who share my food plan or Higher Power or any other aspect of life. All I need to know about a person who comes to OA is that he or she is a compulsive overeater. That tells it all.

> ALL I NEED TO KNOW ABOUT A PERSON WHO COMES TO OA IS THAT HE OR SHE IS A COMPULSIVE OVEREATER.

In the Big Book story entitled, "He who loses his life," the author makes the following statement about the AA philosophy: "I have seen that there is only one law, the law of love, and there are only two sins; the first is to interfere with the growth of another human being, and the second is to interfere with one's own growth." I hope and pray that OA can adopt that philosophy as its own.

Overland Park, Kansas

INSEPARABLE SOLUTION

"**W**rite an article for *Lifeline*." I kept hearing that phrase in my head. It isn't that I hadn't thought of doing it before, but every time I decided on a topic, I'd see it in the next issue of the magazine!

But there is a subject that has been on my mind lately, and I believe that we cannot say enough about it. That is, the importance of abstinence versus the importance of recovery. Can the two be separated? Can I have one without the other? I don't believe so.

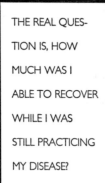

THE REAL QUESTION IS, HOW MUCH WAS I ABLE TO RECOVER WHILE I WAS STILL PRACTICING MY DISEASE?

I hear a lot of talk about this subject in OA in my area. For example, I'd suggested that there be an abstinence requirement for speakers at one of the meetings I go to, which brought up a lot of feelings among members, including one important question: Is the time one has been in the program more important than how much abstinence one has?

I can only speak from my own experience. Please understand that I am not trying to minimize the importance of continuing to attend meetings and of working the program to the best of one's ability even if one is not presently abstaining. I attended OA meetings for ten years before I was able to abstain on a continuous basis. Had I not kept coming back, who knows where I would be today. The real question is, how much was I able to recover while I was still practicing my disease?

At the end of step one in the AA *Twelve Steps and Twelve Traditions*, it states, "Practicing AA's remaining eleven steps means the adoption of attitudes and actions that almost no alcoholic who is still drinking can dream of taking." Is this any less true for the compulsive overeater? I don't believe so. Isn't my recovery dependent on the adoption of certain spiritual principles, and don't I need to work the steps to accomplish that? Yes!

My first ten years in the program were a struggle, to say the least. Yes, I did make progress, but slowly. Now, after abstaining for more than twelve years, I can see the difference between that slow progress and the real progress I have made since beginning to abstain. And the changes have been dramatic.

When food was my god, my world was very limited — emotionally, physically, and spiritually. I went to work, to the market, home, and then to bed. My relationship with my two sons consisted mostly of my yelling at them. I felt so much shame and degradation because I was not able to give them the love and nurturing they needed. I did not perform very well on my job because the obsession with food was so strong. I was not capable of a healthy relationship with a man. I really just wanted someone to love me and take care of me — someone I could control. I had no relationship with God; I was not capable of that because my disease separated me from God.

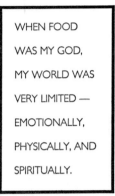

WHEN FOOD WAS MY GOD, MY WORLD WAS VERY LIMITED — EMOTIONALLY, PHYSICALLY, AND SPIRITUALLY.

All of the above was a part of my first ten years in OA. What has changed in the last dozen years, you might ask? Well, just about everything!

Today, my sons and I have a very open relationship. The transformation began when I stopped spanking them. With that, their fear of me lessened. Then I found I could talk to them in a normal tone of voice. We started to love one another. I was also helped by several kind and loving people who pointed out the error of some of my ways. Because those people told me lovingly — and because I was not eating — I came to see what they were talking about, and thus changed my actions. I stayed abstinent through many difficult years, and I am happy to say that I and my sons, who are now eighteen and twenty years old, are now on the other side.

At one time, I was unable to perform on a job because of my obsession with food. With abstinence came an opportunity for a real career. My self-esteem had been very low in that area, but with each small success, it grew. Today, I am successful in my work. The best part is that I know I am good at what I do, and that I am capable and intelligent. I look and act professionally because I am a professional.

Today, my husband and I have a relationship that I never dreamed was possible or thought I deserved. Six years ago we separated, and all my closest friends thought we were headed for the divorce court. They believed there was no way that our relationship could survive. But we worked hard to make it good, and it has paid off. I abstained through it all. What a miracle.

> THE GREATEST GIFT OF MY ABSTINENCE IS THE FEELING I HAVE KNOWING THAT MY LIFE IS DIRECTED BY GOD.

The biggest change of all — without which I don't believe any of the others would have been possible — is my relationship with God. I know that as long as I make food or any other person, place, or thing my god, I leave no room for a loving Higher Power in my life.

The greatest gift of my abstinence is the feeling I have knowing that my life is directed by God. It is only in retrospect that I can see how God works in my life. Whenever I have a problem or a situation that causes me discomfort, I look back over the years and remind myself that, with God in charge, everything always works out for good, even if I cannot see it at the time.

The Big Book says that we have a daily reprieve based upon the maintenance of our spiritual condition. I have experienced that reprieve because I have been rescued from a deadly disease, one that could surely kill me. I owe my life to God for providing the rescue and for continually showing me the way.

So, how important is my recovery if I am not abstaining? For me, I cannot have one without the other.

San Rafael, California

Two

PRACTICAL WAYS TO
ACHIEVE ABSTINENCE

FINDING A SIMPLE SOLUTION

When I first arrived at OA, I had my own definition of abstinence: not eating. Within my first few meetings, however, I heard a confusing bunch of rules about what abstinence was. I heard it was no refined sugar, no white flour, no fats, no desserts and pastries, or some combination of these restrictions. All I could hear was that I would never have a cookie again, and I wouldn't be able to follow this set of rules at all, much less — as my conditioning demanded — perfectly! As I look back, it's no wonder I gained ten pounds before I became willing to accept the program instead of the rules.

One day I picked up a meeting schedule that included Rozanne S.'s definition of abstinence. There I read something I could do: I could stop eating between breakfast and lunch, between lunch and dinner, and between dinner and breakfast. At least, I told myself, I could do that for one day — so I did. And I kept to that plan and maintained that abstinence for nearly a year, during which time I lost thirty-nine pounds.

> THE DAYS I FEEL ABSTINENT ARE GIFTS FROM MY HIGHER POWER, THOSE GLORIOUS DAYS WHEN I REALIZE I HAVE ONLY EATEN ENOUGH TO SATISFY MY BODY'S NEEDS.

In fact, except for a couple of notable slips, I've been able to maintain that plan. When I lose my abstinence, I gain ten pounds. Today, I know that "three meals a day with nothing in between" is a good food plan for me. Without it, I'd have no physical recovery. But I also know that adherence to a food plan is not freedom from compulsive overeating. When I confuse the two, I open the door to dishonesty, rationalization, and the loss of my program.

The days I feel abstinent are gifts from my Higher Power, those glorious days when I realize I have only eaten enough to satisfy my body's needs. Somehow, I don't notice this when it's happening, which is the greatest gift of all: to be able to go through a period of time without even thinking of food. I pray daily for the willingness to let that kind of abstinence — true freedom from compulsive overeating — happen in my life.

Fair Oaks, California

BUILDING ON A FOUNDATION

S eparating the terms abstinence and food plan has helped me simplify the meaning of abstinence. As OA defines it, abstinence is refraining from compulsive overeating, and my food plan is what helps me refrain. I believe we all have the same abstinence. What differs among us are our food plans.

There have been and continue to be many different food plans in OA. We used to have the "gray sheet" and the "orange sheet." There were seven different plans suggested in the pamphlet *Dignity of Choice*. In 1987, however, the Conference abolished the use of these, contending that "offering food plans at OA meetings is a violation of tradition ten. While each individual OA member is free to choose a personal plan for abstinence, OA as a whole cannot print, endorse, or distribute food plan information to members." Even though OA eliminated its own food plans, they are still a vital part of members' recovery. Today some of us seek plans from medical professionals, while others allow one to develop over a period of time, often by trial and error.

> AS OA DEFINES IT, ABSTINENCE IS REFRAINING FROM COMPULSIVE OVEREATING, AND MY FOOD PLAN IS WHAT HELPS ME REFRAIN.

I have been abstaining from compulsive overeating for sixteen years, and my abstinence has stayed constant. I haven't binged or exhibited the behaviors surrounding food that I did when I was compulsively overeating. What has changed several times over the years is my food plan. A hypoglycemic, I began with an appropriate food plan, but when that condition became controllable, I adjusted my plan. Moreover, as I have aged and my physical needs have shifted, I've modified my plan accordingly.

I've heard members say they dislike the term abstinence because it has a negative connotation for them. When they "lost" or "broke" their abstinence, they felt ashamed and judged. Before I distinguished between abstinence and a food plan, I felt the same way. If I deviated, even slightly, from my food plan, I felt guilty. Many people told me I had "slipped" and needed to start over. Thus began a ten-year cycle of starting, "slipping," and starting over. Finally, when I moved, I discovered members here use the term "slip" to mean a deviation from one's food plan. What a relief! A "slip" no longer meant a break in my abstinence.

> IF I DEVIATED, EVEN SLIGHTLY, FROM MY FOOD PLAN, I FELT GUILTY. MANY PEOPLE TOLD ME I HAD "SLIPPED" AND NEEDED TO START OVER.

My current abstinence began at that point — the point I decided never to "start over" again. This doesn't mean I give myself permission to binge. It means I don't have to be perfect with my food; and giving up this perfection has enabled me to abstain for the past sixteen years. I now acknowledge that I make mistakes. I am human. I am a compulsive overeater.

I also learned I had to establish my abstinence from wherever I was. Whereas some overeaters cannot go from bingeing to a rigid food plan, others must have that rigidity to begin. For me, a strict food plan was a prescription for failure because I felt I could never do it perfectly. I realized I had to define a successful day of abstinence and build on that. So I asked myself, "What is the best I can do today and feel I've been abstinent at the end of the day?" Upon formulating my own answer to that question — everyone could answer differently — I followed that plan. And when I went to sleep that first night, I felt I had succeeded, which made the next day that much easier. I began building these successful days one upon the other.

As time has passed, the road has gotten narrower. What felt

okay yesterday may not work today, so I make the necessary changes in my food plan. That doesn't mean I failed yesterday or "broke" my abstinence. On the contrary, it means I am learning through abstaining. Because I am abstinent, I am more in touch with my Higher Power and more aware of the changes needed in my plan. I can also detect now when the problem isn't food, but something else I need to look at. It doesn't mean I'm bad. It means I'm human, and it reminds me I'm a compulsive overeater.

Abstinence is the most important thing in my life today. Without it, I give up all the gifts my Higher Power and program have given me: sanity, love, friendship, peace, laughter, and joy. My food plan allows me to abstain comfortably. If it stops working for me, I can change it and still be abstinent. Likewise, I'm comfortable with the definition of abstinence. It has arms big enough to hold all of us. It unifies us, which is the essence of the first tradition.

GOING TO EXTREMES

Abstinence for me is not merely the act of refraining from compulsive overeating. If I could have done that, I would never have needed OA meetings and tools. I had given up trying long before I came here. It wasn't until I took extreme measures that I was able to live free from the compulsion to overeat or eat compulsively.

In my opinion, OA's definition of abstinence is inadequate; it lends itself to many different interpretations. Its ambiguity has led to confusion and discord among the Fellowship. Sadly, I have seen members struggling to define their own abstinence while harming their bodies in the process. I've heard them claim their abstinence is not eating fast food, not eating while driving, not watching TV or reading while eating, not eating one particular food, only eating when hungry, or not eating after six o'clock. This sounds like the kind of insanity that brought me to

OA in the first place.

When I came to believe that the disease of compulsive overeating was a serious, unrelenting, and progressive illness, I understood that extreme measures are required for ongoing recovery. For me, extreme measures meant giving up the foods that were keeping me in my disease. Sugar, alcohol, flour, caffeine, fried foods, fatty foods, and other personal binge foods are no longer part of my life. Extreme measures also meant following a defined food plan, so now I eat my meals at specified time intervals, and I weigh and measure all of my portions, even in restaurants.

> FOR ME, EXTREME MEASURES MEANT GIVING UP THE FOODS THAT WERE KEEPING ME IN MY DISEASE.

For ongoing recovery, abstinence needs to be the most important thing in my life without exception. I believe I need to be abstinent while working and living the steps. This gives me the clarity to see myself for who I really am; when I was overeating, I couldn't see past the first bite. Abstinence lifts me out of my self-will and brings me in line with God's will. It's God's will for me to abstain so that I can live my life to the fullest.

Consequently, abstinence means not only refraining from the act of compulsive overeating, but also eating proper portions, following sound nutritional guidelines, and refraining from foods that keep me in my disease. Abstinence means changing behaviors and attitudes concerning food. Abstinence means surrender.

I believe this definition of abstinence can work for everyone. I've abstained this way one day at a time for sixteen months. I have released 100 pounds, I'm now at goal weight, and I've achieved a level of serenity and happiness I've never known. For someone who was so deep in the clutches of this disease, it's truly a miracle I have found my way out. But miracles happen every day in OA, and if it can happen to me, it can happen to anyone.

San Jose, California

EMPLOYING THE NUMBER ONE TOOL

Abstinence is a tool of the program which some people use and some do not. Abstinence and my Higher Power are the most important things in my life. They work together hand in hand.

I've been abstinent for more than two years and am maintaining a significant weight loss. I'm very committed to my abstinence. Without it I wouldn't be clear enough to face the challenges of my life. I believe one has to put the substance down and keep it down to work this program effectively. But abstinence is a very personal issue. The foods I eat may or may not be suitable for someone else. We have to find an abstinence which works for us. I must admit that I'm disturbed when I hear someone trying to tell another person what food plan to use. As we are repeatedly told, OA is not a diet club. This is about much larger issues than having the right food plan.

I don't think there's a right or wrong way to approach working the steps. Some people start working the steps and become abstinent. Others get abstinent and then work the steps. The important thing is to work them!

In AA everyone puts down the same substance. In OA there is a great deal of controversy over certain foods. Just as we had our own styles when it came to compulsive overeating, we each have to find our own style in abstinence. We can get suggestions from other people, but ultimately we have to look within and do what feels right for us.

> I DON'T THINK THERE'S A RIGHT OR WRONG WAY TO APPROACH WORKING THE STEPS.

I have a simple, healthy manner of eating. This works for me, but I never ever tell anyone that my way is the best way, and that he or she should eat what I eat.

My abstinence has everything to do with working the steps, especially, but not exclusively, the first three. I've put abstinence in my Higher Power's hands. That doesn't mean that I don't ever think about food. Food is my drug, and when anything happens in my life, food thoughts can float around my mind, but that's where they stay. I continue to abstain from compulsive overeating until the thoughts pass. I use all the tools of the program to help me through.

In order for me to grow spiritually and work the steps the best I can, I need to be abstinent. I was an insane individual when I was compulsively overeating. Thanks to abstinence I'm also able to really look at myself and my behavior and determine what is going on — if I owe an amends, if I'm resentful, or if I'm being controlling. I'm also able to experience all of my feelings.

I THINK WE ALL NEED TO ACCEPT ONE ANOTHER IN OA.

I think we all need to accept one another in OA. That doesn't mean everyone likes everyone else, but there has to be a certain mutual respect. We are all linked by a common bond: the desire to stop eating compulsively. Exactly how each of us attains this is an individual matter, just as each one of us defines our Higher Power differently. We are supposed to be a Fellowship, and we need to strive for unity, instead of dividing into separate little groups according to what foods we choose to eat. That defeats the whole purpose.

New York, New York

CHOOSING WITH PERSONAL FREEDOM

Abstinence has been defined in simple terms — the action of refraining from compulsive overeating — yet we tend to complicate the definition with our personal views. Too often we hear that abstinence means no sugar, flour, or even caffeine. It's wonderful that some members have identified these substances as dangerous for them and are successful in eliminating them from their diets. It should be stressed, however, that these are personal decisions, not right or even beneficial for everyone in OA. People who have no problem with a particular food should not feel pressured or have to endure shocked looks for their food choices.

I think this is particularly harmful to newcomers who may be scared off by the thought of never eating sugar or flour again. They need to understand that food is not our problem — the compulsive behavior is. And compulsive is not *what* we eat, it's *how*. As we begin working the program, we are soon capable of discerning the difference between eating out of compulsion or simple hunger. Then what or when we eat becomes secondary to whether the eating is healthy or is driven by our disease. If we try to compare ourselves to or copy others, we may fail to live up to the standard and react with a binge. Why give newcomers any more guilt, fear, or pressure than they have when they come in the door?

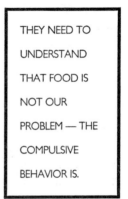

THEY NEED TO UNDERSTAND THAT FOOD IS NOT OUR PROBLEM — THE COMPULSIVE BEHAVIOR IS.

Let's give OAs, both oldtimers and newcomers, a basic definition of abstinence and allow them to make their own choices. Thus everyone can have the same abstinence, although some will limit food intake more than others and individual food plans may change over time. When we are abstinent, the action of refraining will be present regardless of what we eat. Just as OA promises us freedom from compulsive overeating, we should give fellow members the freedom to shape their specific abstinence and make their own wonderful journey to recovery.

Crestview, Florida

RELAPSE PREVENTION

I've been abstaining in OA for over eleven years, maintaining a 110-pound weight loss for ten of them. Although none of us is cured and there's always the threat of relapse, the miracle of OA is that relapse is not inevitable. OA has given me and countless others a way of life that works.

When I first got abstinent, I was scared of relapse. My life before OA had been one of constant "relapse" with a few transitory stretches of almost successful dieting. At last I'd found something that seemed to work, and I was scared of people in relapse, afraid that their troubles with food might be contagious and lead me back to destructive eating.

As my sponsor wisely pointed out, however, I didn't have to worry about catching the disease of compulsive overeating — I already had it.

My sponsor pointed out that in OA we recover by working with other compulsive overeaters, and that includes those in relapse. He suggested that working closely with these people' would help me learn from their mistakes without having to repeat them myself.

What are some of those mistakes? One of the most common precursors to relapse is insufficient attendance at OA meetings. It's been my observation that those who attend frequently and do service seem to relapse less than those who attend infrequently. Sometimes we've come so far that we think we're cured and no longer need OA meetings.

ONE OF THE MOST COMMON PRECURSORS TO RELAPSE IS INSUFFICIENT ATTENDANCE AT OA MEETINGS.

Other common mistakes involve not using one or more of the tools, or not working all of the steps. A person might try to get by without a commitment to a service position or without writing a fourth-step inventory. Working all the steps and using all the tools doesn't mean a life without food problems, but not working the program will guarantee them.

To watch a close OA friend go through this painful experience is distressing. A relapse takes on a life of its own, with temporary moments of hope followed by painful demoralization. Sometimes it seems as if nothing will end it. But relapses burn themselves out sooner or later. They may end faster for those who attend lots of OA meetings, but they never end quickly enough.

I admit that I'm powerless over food — and that includes other people's food as well. There's nothing I can do to guarantee that others will stay abstinent, but I can pray for them, talk to them, and offer rides to meetings. I try not to offer advice unless asked, since I know how I hate it when others give it to me.

Here's what I do to stay abstinent: Every morning, I ask God for help, and then take a few moments of quiet time and meditate. I call my sponsor almost every day, and I sponsor several people.

I attend about five OA meetings a week. It's easy for me to eat properly when I get to a lot of meetings and harder when I don't. I have a service position at a meeting, which makes it more likely that I'll show up. My phone calling, reading, and writing are more sporadic, but over the course of a month I'll use all the tools.

I eat the same number of meals a day, and I pay close attention to portion size. I don't eat foods that cause problems for me, including some that others in program are able to handle.

At night I do a mental tenth-step inventory and remind myself that my disease is threefold: physical, emotional, and spiritual. I then ask myself where I am physically, emotionally, and spiritually to identify what areas in my life need attention.

I keep a big margin of safety in my program. I don't ever want to return to the living hell of compulsive overeating and morbid obesity.

Arlington, Virginia

CONDITION CHECK

I've heard people speak about sloppy abstinence ever since I've been in the OA program. I never cared much for that term. I felt that if one set down a plan of abstinence, one either stuck to it or one didn't. Certainly that was the case for me.

Now my abstinence has gotten sloppy. I haven't relapsed, but there's a real risk of my doing just that. Suddenly I realize that I have to eat some of my own words — and they're not on my food plan!

I've come face-to-face with my powerlessness. I don't want to admit to myself that I'm still powerless. I've been in program for several years now, and I should be getting it right. I haven't been doing the things I said I wouldn't do with my eating, and thus haven't specifically broken my abstinence. Still the obsession with food has been sneaking back in.

I always expected that relapse, if it came, would come with a crash — but instead it appears to be creeping in, little by little. In a way, that's good — with God's help, I can stop it before it gets out of hand, but a "creeping" relapse may be more difficult to recognize.

> I'VE COME FACE-TO-FACE WITH MY POWERLESSNESS. I DON'T WANT TO ADMIT TO MYSELF THAT I'M STILL POWERLESS.

After the discussion of step ten in the Big Book (page 84) it says, "by this time sanity will have returned. . . . If tempted, we recoil . . . as from a hot flame. We react sanely and normally, and we will find that this has happened automatically." This promise was granted to me for a long time, but lately I've found that more often than not it hasn't been the case.

Why was this promise fulfilled in my life and then, to a degree at least, taken from me? I find the answer in the next paragraph. "We are not cured . . . . What we really have is a daily reprieve contingent on the maintenance of our spiritual condition." Clearly my spiritual condition must be lacking.

I've looked at the things I did when I first came into the program and what I'm doing now, and I notice that I've selectively stopped doing some of those things. For instance, I used to pray regularly; I now pray intermittently. I learned to meditate and now rarely do. I was strict with my food plan and my abstinence; I'm now much looser. I exercised regularly; I don't any longer. I wrote daily; lately, it's several times a month. I used to read program literature every day; now I do it when I get the time, maybe once every week or two. I suppose what I'm realizing is that these efforts aren't sufficient for me to remain in fit spiritual condition.

I tend to see things in black-and-white terms: I'm either abstinent or I'm not, I'm either working my program or I'm not. This is false. I'm still abstinent by my own definition, even though my abstinence hasn't been as clean as I'd like. I've been working my program, but not to the degree that I need to.

I'm still sponsoring and doing lots of service, and I'm of some help to those who still suffer. I'm still reading literature, making phone calls, writing, and getting to a good many meetings. So where do I go from here?

> I MET WITH MY SPONSOR AND WROTE OUT A PLAN OF ACTION THAT I FELT WOULD HELP ME.

I met with my sponsor and wrote out a plan of action that I felt would help me. It set reasonable goals for me to work toward, specifically in the areas of food plans, writing, reading, meditation, and exercise. My sponsor also suggested a couple of other areas to work on that I hadn't thought of. He emphasized to me that whatever happens now, and whether or not I accomplish it, is totally up to God. First, I must surrender completely to God. Then I need to do what I can to regain my fit spiritual condition.

I look forward to getting back into that place where I can feel good about myself and get back to losing weight. When and if I do, the credit will go to God, my Higher Power.

San Antonio, Texas

PLUGGING THE DAM

Three weeks ago I found myself in relapse again. My eating was out of control and I felt as if I were drowning in food. The scariest part was that I had no idea when or why it started. I didn't make a conscious decision to start using the food again; it just happened. But I'd stopped doing my footwork and I hadn't been to an OA meeting in a month due to a vacation — and cockiness. My abstinence had been going so well — what did I need a meeting for?

What I did was like taking my finger out of a hole in a dam. The hole got bigger and bigger as I decided it was okay to eat certain foods that weren't a part of my abstinence; in other words, my binge foods. Eventually the dam burst, and I was awash in food.

The sick part of my brain took over. I had trouble remembering that I had a disease. If I could eat "just one" of a certain binge food, my thinking went, then surely I was a normal eater. Now I know that the "controlled eating" of "just one" leads to the uncontrolled eating of many more. Eventually my abstinence is gone and I'm back into my illness.

> NOW I KNOW THAT THE "CONTROLLED EATING" OF "JUST ONE" LEADS TO THE UNCONTROLLED EATING OF MANY MORE.

This relapse scared me enough to examine why I couldn't or wouldn't turn my abstinence and program over to my Higher Power. I asked myself: "What have I got to lose by believing that a power greater than myself can take my food addiction and restore me to sanity?" My answer: I'd lose the food, how I wanted to eat it and when.

I realized then just how strong my illness is. I wasn't willing to give up the food and had decided that I wouldn't like the new life my H.P. would make for me. I understood how sick it was to decide I didn't want to be restored to sanity and abstinence because I thought I knew what the outcome would be. In reality I have no idea what recovery will be like. I know it can't be worse than the pain and insanity of this last relapse.

I prayed for willingness and decided I had nothing to lose — except excess food — by believing my H.P. could and would restore me to sanity. I became willing to make daily food plans and call them in to my food sponsor.

At this point I'd been in OA a year and had never been willing to call in my food before. I enjoyed deciding what I wanted to eat right before my meals. I realized that I'd gotten a lot of excitement from eating what I wanted right at the moment, but the willingness to call in my food came from my H.P.

This has been a hard year. After my first seven days of abstinence I remembered that I'd been an incest victim as a child. For a long time I used my pain as an excuse to overeat, with the rationale that I had to use anything I could to get through these painful, fearful days.

Reading "Journey Through Deception" in the Brown Book helped me more than I can say. It taught me that, if I want to get well, I can't use the pain of my childhood as an excuse to overeat. Food doesn't help the pain — it buries it. To recover, I must feel all of my feelings; to do that, I must be abstinent.

I'm willing to go to any length to remain abstinent. I'm going to OA meetings, reading OA literature every day, and talking with my food sponsor every night. I'm still scared of relapse, so I'm praying to my H.P. and continuing to turn my will and my life over every day.

Athens, Georgia

TRAVEL INSURANCE

I love to travel and am blessed to have the opportunity to take many trips each year. Because I am a compulsive overeater, however, traveling offers me extra challenges on the road to recovery.

In the past, a trip had been an excuse to overeat, and I often gained large amounts of weight while away from home. But since working the OA program of recovery, I can travel and maintain my abstinence and weight. I would like to share some of the methods that have worked for me.

■ Get meeting lists and contact members. Long before I leave home, I write to the World Service Office to obtain a list of meetings and contacts for the area I'm visiting. It's always gratifying to see the program in action in other places and to feel the familiar OA warmth in an unfamiliar area.

- Find out what the "food scene" will be like ahead of time. If it's a business meeting I'm going to, I call to ask whether pre-set breakfasts or lunches will be included, and, if so, what foods will be served. If I'm visiting a friend, I politely but honestly make my food needs known before I arrive. After getting as much information as I can, I make up a food plan with my sponsor. Sometimes this plan includes a commitment to eat a little differently than I would at home.

- Plan ahead for airline travel. Before I fly, I carefully think through my meals. I almost always bring my own lunch, and sometimes my own supper. That way I'm assured I'll eat foods that are healthy for me. If there are delays, I can still eat my meals at regular times.

- If possible, prepare your own meals. On vacations, my husband and I try to stay at places that have kitchens. That way, we can have breakfast "at home" and take a picnic lunch with us. Besides helping me stay abstinent and avoid so many restaurant meals, it's fun!

- Take program literature along. I take a supply of OA literature with me, especially *Lifeline*, because it's small and easy to pack.

- Keep in touch with your sponsor. My sponsor has received calls from many faraway places! Sometimes we set a telephone date so that I'll be sure to reach her.

- Keep a food journal. While traveling, I write down what I eat and any feelings I may be having about my food. When I get home, I give this journal to my sponsor to read. I like knowing that someone will know how I ate — both on the days that I felt good about my food and on the days I felt shaky.

- Be flexible. And that brings me to the last but possibly most important aspect of traveling abstinently: remember to be flexible — accept food situations that are beyond one's control. I need to be extra kind and, above all, forgiving of myself if I eat differently than I'd eat at home.

OA teaches me to live in the world. Although I can never forget that I have the disease of compulsive overeating, I've found that I can experience the joys of traveling as I continue to recover.

Chapel Hill, North Carolina

DESIGN FOR LIVING

I attended my first OA meeting four years ago just wanting to lose twenty pounds. I was a slow learner. Three months later I finally got a sponsor and embarked on the path of recovery. Abstinence was hard. I wanted it to be easy. I'd be abstinent for as long as sixty or even ninety days, then I'd feel I deserved to bust out and do what I wanted: eat the foods I wanted, in the amounts I wanted, when I wanted them. The only thing I could really manage to do was to keep coming back to meetings.

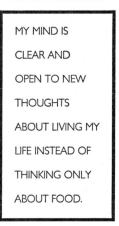

MY MIND IS CLEAR AND OPEN TO NEW THOUGHTS ABOUT LIVING MY LIFE INSTEAD OF THINKING ONLY ABOUT FOOD.

Two years later I became convinced that I was one of those who couldn't recover because I couldn't get abstinent and stay abstinent. Then God put a wonderful woman with sixteen years of abstinence into my life. She suggested that I design an abstinence that I could live with. For me that meant no "banned" foods, and no strict guidelines about what, when, and how I would eat. What a comfort it was to know that I could have the foods I liked in moderate amounts whenever I chose to plan them into a meal.

It is now two years since that time, and I'll shortly have two years of abstinence. The obsession with eating has been lifted. My mind is clear and open to new thoughts about living my life instead of thinking only about food. I plan outings with friends and family, go to movies, the beach, and even restaurants. I can hear when the disease of compulsive overeating is talking to me and I can confront it. No more the victim role for me!

I'm grateful to that wonderful woman and to all the people in

OA who share their experience in confronting this disease, the strength which their fellowship gives me, and the hope that I can share the OA way of life forever.

San Diego, California

CRYSTAL CLEAR

Last year we had a family get-together in Sacramento and went to the zoo and the museum. We had a picnic lunch in the park and my mother-in-law brought some cupcakes. I didn't have one, but after everyone else ate all they wanted, there were several left over. She gave them to me, and I quickly bundled them into the car.

The next day during the trip home, I noticed them and offered them to the kids to finish off. I wanted one (or ten) quite a bit, so I was relieved to see them all eaten up — or so I thought.

My youngest ate about half of his, including the icing, then gripping it in his hand for a while, he fell asleep in his car seat. The cupcake fell on the floor of the car. When we stopped to stretch a couple of hours later, I helped him out of his car seat and picked up the half-eaten, dirty, stale cupcake. Instead of throwing it away as I had meant to, I stuffed it into my mouth.

When I told an OA friend this story to illustrate how sick I continue to be, she told me about a very expensive and beautiful crystal bowl she and her husband were given for a wedding present. It was too valuable to be used every day, so it was put away for special occasions.

One day, when she was dusting, she carelessly dropped a cheap ceramic bowl on it and helplessly watched her priceless crystal shatter into a thousand pieces.

She tied the two stories together — my abstinence was the precious crystal and the dirty cupcake was the ceramic bowl. Did I want to break my priceless abstinence for a piece of trash? This symbolic mental image has stuck with me and helped me through quite a few rough spots. As much as I may want to eat a particular something, it isn't worth it; my abstinence is much too valuable to me to break so carelessly.

Susanville, California

TIME-TESTED RECOVERY

At three o'clock in the morning on the Saturday after Thanksgiving I could not get to sleep. I felt horrible because of the bingeing I had done for the previous two days, and I was scared. For some time I have been struggling emotionally with a special relationship in my life that is not going the way I had hoped. This relationship has been on my mind constantly, and I've been afraid of what the outcome will be. Feeling very powerless and frustrated, I used the holiday as an excuse to overeat.

I've been in the program a little over six years and am maintaining a 341-pound weight loss. My program is strong, but for those few days I didn't work it, nor did I trust my Higher Power. What I experienced was a major slip for me, and it brought back a flood of bad memories.

> WHEN I WAS GROWING UP I REMEMBER TURNING TO FOOD FOR COMFORT WHENEVER I WAS AFRAID.

When I was growing up I remember turning to food for comfort whenever I was afraid. Since I felt inadequate, the fear of failure was ever present. I came into OA weighing 521 pounds; I was unemployed, divorced, and very desperate. I felt I had failed at everything in life, especially as a son, husband, and father. I did not want to live anymore but was too scared to do anything about it. It didn't take me long to realize that this program was exactly what I needed, so I surrendered myself to it.

My Higher Power and the loving, caring people in this program helped me to start facing the mountain of fear I had built up inside me without having to turn to food for sustenance.

With every meeting I went to, every tool I used, every step I worked, and every prayer I prayed, I was gaining strength and courage. The miracle of my recovery was beginning.

Food is cunning, baffling, and powerful. I turned to it over this past Thanksgiving holiday in order to cope with the fear I was feeling. It didn't help, of course, it never does — it just made a bad situation worse.

I have finally managed to turn that special relationship over to my Higher Power and will accept the outcome, whatever it is. I feel a great deal of relief and my abstinence has returned. Writing this article has helped too.

One thing that keeps getting stronger as my recovery progresses is the knowledge that no matter how much I may be hurting or how bad things may seem at times, as long as I maintain contact with my Higher Power and this beautiful program, I will be okay no matter what comes along. This has been proven to me time and time again throughout my recovery.

Racine, Wisconsin

IT'S ALL IN THE STEPS

I learned the importance of working the twelve suggested steps of recovery — the hard way. When my first sponsor in Alcoholics Anonymous proposed that I use the fourth and fifth steps to "clean house," I refused.

"I'm a Jesuit priest," I told him. "All I have ever done since I began studying for the priesthood is go to confession."

How wrong I was. I did not want to admit that my physical addiction was only a symptom of an underlying mental and spiritual illness. For five years I was a "dry drunk" with a two-step program: 1) I stopped drinking; and 2) I bragged about it. Failure to confront the exact nature of my wrongs kept me trapped in my character defects, and I simply switched from active alcoholism to compulsive overeating.

I reached the point of wanting to die. Suicide was not an option because I didn't think it would look good on my resume.

Another Jesuit, a recovering alcoholic, finally sold me on the fourth and fifth steps as the key to acquiring the restoration to sanity that the second step promises. I worked those two steps with him and was granted a marvelous sense of belonging to the Fellowship of those who are in recovery.

Working the fourth and fifth steps helped me to recognize that I was an egomaniac with an inferiority complex. In other twelve-step programs, I dealt with the origins of my depression and low self-esteem by sharing experience, strength, and hope with other adult children of alcoholics. On my first program anniversary, I told a friend how grateful I was that my feelings of uselessness and self-pity were beginning to disappear, even though I was still carrying around the extra 44 pounds I had gained while I was depressed.

> ONE OF MY CHIEF CONVICTIONS ABOUT THE STEPS IS THAT THERE ARE MANY DIFFERENT WAYS TO WORK THEM.

I think I expected my friend to pat me on the back, tell me I didn't look so bad, and give me the latest and greatest diet she had found. Instead she said, "Go to Overeaters Anonymous. They know about compulsive overeating."

I resisted for a few weeks, but a Labor Day binge proved to me once again that it was insane for me to think that I could cure myself. Two days later I went to my first OA meeting and began working the steps all over again with a new group of fellow sufferers. After two years I have shared a fifth step twice and am planning to do so again. I have lost forty-two pounds and have taken eight inches off my waist. More importantly, I have gained some wisdom and serenity that help me to "live life on life's terms."

One of my chief convictions about the steps is that there are many different ways to work them. After all, if we can each have a God according to our own understanding, may we not also work the steps accordingly?

Some people like to view the steps on a medical model: the first three are "intensive care," steps four to nine are "inpatient treatment," and then we are healthy enough to work the last three steps on our own. Others emphasize working the steps in order. I once heard someone say that working the first step is being in first grade, which would make those working the twelfth step seniors in the "school of recovery." To this way of thinking, the first step is something that we get farther and farther away from the more we journey in recovery.

My own imperfect experience in recovery suggests that it is best for me to see how all twelve steps continue to work together to keep me on the path toward health and happiness. In the other models, going back to the first step might feel like failure. We are liable to feel that we have "flunked out" of the higher grades and have been sent back to learn a lesson that we should not have forgotten, or that we are going backwards to square one, losing all the forward progress we thought we had made.

For me, it works best to think of each step as support for all the others so that I am not ashamed or dismayed when I find that I need more of the wisdom available in the first step in order to carry on with the ninth.

> A MORAL INVEN-
> TORY (STEP
> FOUR) ENABLES
> ME TO ADMIT
> THE NATURE OF
> MY WRONGS
> (STEP FIVE).

The first step serves me as gasoline does an automobile: I draw regularly on the reservoir of acceptance of my powerlessness, but have to stop from time to time to fill up again on the insight that I will never save myself from the "bondage of self." The first step is the foundation of all the other steps, even when I am not conscious of the support it offers me.

Steps two to nine seem to me to work in pairs. For example, belief in a benevolent Higher Power (step two) enables me to turn myself over to the care of that Power (step three). A moral inventory (step four) enables me to admit the nature of my wrongs (step five). Readiness to change (step six) makes it possible for me to let go of my shortcomings (step seven). The list of those I have harmed (step eight) guides me in deciding how to make amends (step nine). As I work the initial step in each of these pairs, I do so knowing there is a follow-through in the next step.

The last three steps are very special to me. Although I believe that it's best to work all the steps in order, I do not see how I could have postponed working these last three steps until I had finished making amends.

The tenth step is something I did daily from day one. It encouraged me to keep my current affairs clean while I labored to "clear away the wreckage" of my past. Similarly, I couldn't work any of the steps in a healthy fashion without conscious contact with my Higher Power. I use each of the steps as a topic for prayer and meditation. I know that this is a spiritual program, and every step is spiritual if I allow the light of the eleventh step to fill all the rest.

> RECOGNIZING HOW THEY ALL WORK TOGETHER HELPS ME DO WHAT I NEED MOST FOR MY RECOVERY.

The first part of the twelfth step seems to confirm this view for me: each step contributes to my spiritual awakening. I didn't wait until I had finished working all the steps before sharing my joy of recovery with others, nor do I want others to wait. As Bill W. discovered by helping Dr. Bob, carrying the message is essential to recovery. To me, everyone who shares at a meeting is working the second part of the twelfth step, even if all one can say is, "I need help" or "Food has me beaten again."

Understanding how the steps work together in my recovery doesn't mean I pick and choose among them, substituting one I like for another that I don't like. Recognizing how they all work together helps me do what I need most for my recovery.

Syracuse, New York

FORMULA FOR LIVING

With God's grace, I've had five and one-half years of clear and clean abstinence. For a person who couldn't go one day without bingeing for up to three hours, this is nothing less than a miracle!

Coming into the program, I accepted the first step in its entirety. I still do. I know with all my heart that I am powerless over food, and that taking the first compulsive bite will return me to a life marked by despair, low self-esteem, poor health, and a fat body.

Even more impressive than the gift of abstinence is the fact that I now live comfortably without excess food. All the credit for that goes to the remaining eleven steps of the Overeaters Anonymous twelve-step program.

For years it seemed as if I couldn't get full no matter how much I ate. I've come to see that food could never fill the void I had; it was a spiritual sustenance that I needed. By working the steps, I've tapped into a Power that rests quietly within. Truly, it is a gift of the twelve steps.

Besides the twelve steps, another guide I live by is a little formula my sponsor taught me: E + R = 0. The event plus my response equals the outcome.

Before my recovery began, I responded to most events by overeating. Relationships, jobs, vacations, health problems — all were dealt with by compulsive eating. And the outcome was always the same — remorse, fear, and pain.

The E + R = 0 formula showed me that I needed to learn healthier responses to life and its events. Today, prayer is my first response to any uncertain situation in my life. That is followed by action, which may be to call a sponsor, go to a meeting, write, wait, or talk to the people involved.

When I follow the formula, I feel positive about the outcome.

Now, I resolve my problems by practicing the principles of the program and by utilizing my sponsor's formula. That isn't to say I don't have difficult times, but I do always have tools to deal with whatever life presents.

Being abstinent, thin, healthy, and full of life is a direct result of the Overeaters Anonymous program. It is teaching me to stand in the light, where the nourishment I need is always available.

Corona del Mar, California

AUSSIE "HOW-TO"

My name is K. and I'm a compulsive overeater. Although I am Australian, I attended my first OA meeting in Chicago in 1981. I had been en route to California after a stop in Europe to hook up with my sister.

Unfortunately for her (she is not a compulsive overeater), she ended up travelling with me through the last four horrific months of my compulsive overeating.

I thought of nothing but food. I was bad tempered, bossy, rude, selfish, and domineering. I was the older sister so I got away with it. On the last stage of our journey back across the United States, I put "us" on a diet. We were allowed to eat only crackers, cheese, and apples. Since I was driving the car, my sister had no choice; I simply would not stop to allow her out of the car to eat.

I THOUGHT OF NOTHING BUT FOOD. I WAS BAD TEMPERED, BOSSY, RUDE, SELFISH, AND DOMINEERING.

Years later she told me how she'd snuck into shops when we stopped for gas and would have a snack to keep from being hungry all the time.

When we reached California I started going to OA meetings again. Thank God, I got abstinent from the beginning. After eighteen continuous days of abstinence, I felt great. I was so proud of myself that the good feeling didn't leave me for months. I don't mean that it wasn't hard work or that it didn't require enormous effort and discipline on my part, but I felt good.

Initially, I used all sorts of tricks to avoid overeating. I established a strict timetable for my meals. Breakfast was at 7:00 AM. I couldn't get up until then because I had to eat as soon as I got out of bed (most of the time I still do). Lunch was at noon. I'd start watching the clock at about 11:00 AM, convinced I was starving, all the while praying for help. Dinner was at 5:00 PM — sometimes slightly later if I could force myself to cook slowly. By 8:30 PM, I'd have to go to bed, because if I got hungry again, I didn't know if I could trust myself not to have that first compulsive bite.

Later on, when the obsession with mealtimes had passed and I would find myself thinking "food" at an inappropriate time, I'd use little tricks to postpone the act of compulsive overeating. I'd say to myself, "Well, first I'll have a cup of coffee. If I'm still hungry after that, then I can have something." Generally, by the time I made the coffee and drank it, the compulsion to eat would have passed and I'd be OK. I had a whole store of those phrases that started with the word *just*. For example: "Just water the plants, take a bath, ring a friend, wash the dishes, hang out the wash." These phrases really helped me to learn self-discipline.

Another great help to me was identifying the emotions and situations which triggered my compulsion. I divided a sheet of paper into three columns, listing (1) when I felt like eating, (2) what my feelings were at the time, and (3) what kind of character defects I felt provoked the situation. For example, when I had visitors or when I attended social gatherings, I usually felt ill at ease, and I saw my character defect as self-centeredness. My list went on and on.

After I examined the list, I saw that "felt uneasy" came up in nearly every situation. From then on, whenever I thought I was hungry in a situation which made me feel uncomfortable, I would tell myself that it was not hunger I was feeling, but uneasiness. And I knew food would not cure that. Then I made a choice — either I could avoid such situations, or gradually, through working the steps, I could improve my self-esteem and learn to handle them.

And guess what — I have been abstinent now for four continuous years. The obsession with food is gone, the compulsions are few and far between, and thanks to the OA program and OA friends, I have the tools to handle problems when they do arise. My experience has taught me never to underestimate my need for OA meetings and for contact with other members.

Best of all, when I am abstinent, I know I am much closer to God.

Tweed Heads South, Australia

Three

THE SEARCH FOR ABSTINENCE

THE MOMENT IT CLICKED

I attended my first meeting on March 1, 1976. I was desperate. Over many years, I had lost a total of eighty-five pounds, but had recently gained twenty-seven — while on a diet!

That night I heard the only requirement for membership is a desire to stop eating compulsively. To be truthful, I didn't have the requirement for membership. I only wanted to be thin. I had accepted I was meant to be miserable and afraid and couldn't do all the things that "normal" people seemed to do so easily and confidently. I didn't recognize my emotional and spiritual illness at the time, but I knew I needed help with my physical disease.

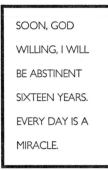

SOON, GOD WILLING, I WILL BE ABSTINENT SIXTEEN YEARS. EVERY DAY IS A MIRACLE.

After eighteen months, even I saw that food plans worked in isolation in OA were no more effective than those I tried on my own. The people at my meeting said, "Stick with the winners." I noticed the winners were those who considered abstinence the most important thing in their lives and who worked the steps.

Finally, on November 13, 1977, I called a sponsor and said I was willing to do whatever I had to do. "Whatever" began with a commitment to follow my food plan, no matter what. This commitment forced me to use the tools and the steps in order to stay abstinent. The tools always got me back on the beam and in a place where I could work a step. Through the twelve steps, my Higher Power worked a miracle — a total rearrangement of thoughts and motives such as the doctor describes in the Big Book. It did not happen quickly. I put many hours into meetings, retreats, and service, but the miracle did begin to take place. For this compulsive overeater, it couldn't have without abstinence from overeating first.

Since then, OA, my abstinence, and my food plan have all changed. I am not the same person I was, yet the framework of OA — the meetings, the steps, the tools, prayer, and meditation — is still what I use to live this life I've been given. And abstaining from compulsive overeating still comes first for me.

I don't know what happened on November 13, 1977. It's best described as an awesome "click," as if a light had come on. My belief system had changed, and I chose to follow it. That first commitment to my food plan not only taught me how to make and keep other commitments, but it also gave me the gift of time — time to work the steps without all the hopelessness, self-hate, and fear of pre-OA life. Soon, God willing, I will be abstinent sixteen years.

Every day is a miracle.

Boulder, Colorado

THE AWARENESS THAT GROWS

Abstinence is a tool. A tool is what I use to get a job done. The job I want to do is to develop noncompulsive eating habits and recover from my disease.

In the beginning, I defined abstinence as a food plan. I developed a personal one primarily by researching nutrition. I wanted food to be a means of keeping my body alive and healthy. I also sought the guidance of a sponsor in establishing my plan. On her advice, I gave up my former binge items. As I continue to follow this plan daily, I'm developing healthy eating habits and achieving continued physical recovery.

IN THE BEGIN-
NING, I DEFINED
ABSTINENCE AS A
FOOD PLAN.

At meetings, I began hearing remarks about eating planned meals in a noncompulsive way, so I expanded my definition. I added the element of "noncompulsive eating" because my compulsion is emotional. Whenever my meals develop into something more than a way to stay alive, I know I have an issue to address. Therefore, my abstinence is also an emotional tool which points out my hidden feelings and helps me recover from compulsive eating. Being aware of my feelings has helped me practice the steps more fully, especially steps four through seven.

Lately, I've discovered abstinence is also a spiritual tool. When I adopted my food plan, I began working the steps. I admitted I was powerless and began relying on a Power greater than myself. As I relied more and more steadily on my H.P., I maintained my abstinence and received the strength to follow my plan. My Higher Power gives me all the things I wanted from food, like love and freedom from inner turmoil.

All these elements — following a food plan, handling my emotions, surrendering my compulsion to a Higher Power — make up my current definition of abstinence. They help me recover.

As a result, I'm able to work and live better. Instead of burying myself in food, I'm open to my surroundings. I've learned I'm more capable and less selfish than I imagined. I've received genuine concern from others and gained a lasting respect for them. I'm at a high level of happiness I thought would never be mine. I'm deeply grateful for this program — I couldn't recover without it.

Richmond, Virginia

LIVING IN THE SOLUTION

Compulsive overeating had completely consumed me by the time I found my way into Overeaters Anonymous. My sole purpose in life was to eat, and at the same time, desperately seek a way to control my weight.

"Why can't I close the refrigerator door?" I'd wonder, tears pouring down my puffy face as I was eating nonstop from the top shelf to the bottom. I wanted to know why, on Saturday nights, when friends were out having fun, I was sitting at home in front of the television eating with both hands, at warp speed. And what sent me back for second, third, and fourth helpings when I wanted to stop at one?

When not actively binge-eating, I was dieting, fasting, or visiting one more doctor, nutritionist, or acupuncturist. I hoped they'd show me the way out of the food, the fat, and my incessant mental and emotional turmoil.

It wasn't until I found Overeaters Anonymous that my insane behavior, thoughts, and feelings began to make sense. That first meeting nearly ten years ago showed me I wasn't alone. There were lots of others just like me who'd lost the power of choice when it came to food.

The men and women in these meetings knew my pain firsthand — they'd lived it. They offered me a road map that led me out of the problem and into the life-giving solution.

"Find a sponsor and a food plan you can follow," they suggested. "Make a commitment to a planned way of eating. Go regularly to meetings. Read the Big Book, The *Twelve Steps of Overeaters Anonymous*, and plenty of other OA literature. Reach out to others through the telephone. Above all, wholeheartedly work the twelve steps."

I couldn't imagine that recovery could hurt more than the torment of compulsive overeating, so I tried it. In the past decade, I've experienced major ups and downs — job changes, deaths, relocations, heartache, and joy — in short, life. But regardless of my degree of discomfort or elation, I've stayed clear of that first bite. I've followed the road map of recovery to the best of my ability, one day at a time. And I've found that living in the solution is the best way to go, under all conditions. Following this map has led me beyond my most heartfelt dreams: I'm healthy, happily married, and at peace with myself and the world around me most of the time. I've just written and published my first book. The love of friends surrounds me. I look forward to the future with an expectation of good. Traveling this road of recovery has shown me that there is a Higher Power — and this power is actively involved in every area of my life.

> IT WASN'T UNTIL I FOUND OVEREATERS ANONYMOUS THAT MY INSANE BEHAVIOR, THOUGHTS, AND FEELINGS BEGAN TO MAKE SENSE.

Positive things happen when I follow our program's directions, keep my feet firmly on the path of God's will, and walk with my head held high into the best that's yet to be.

Corona del Mar, California

TRUST TO THE TEST

My ability to stay abstinent is being severely put to the test. My elderly mother is declining physically and mentally, causing deep concern for my family and me.

There doesn't seem to be a workable solution to allow her to receive proper care and at the same time keep her happy. To her, nothing is right; she sees only the negative.

In praying about the situation I realized that I, too, could easily start seeing only the negative. The more I prayed, the more I

IN TRYING TO TRUST GOD, I FOUND SOME OLD, PAINFUL MEMORIES RISING TO THE SURFACE.

realized I needed to turn this problem over to my Higher Power. But I'm being asked to trust God in a way that scares me. I want to control what happens to me and those I care about. But I can't do it in this situation.

In trying to trust God, I found some old, painful memories rising to the surface. My feelings were telling me to eat, that somehow I'd feel better. Instead I chose to talk my feelings out with someone I knew would listen without giving me a lot of advice. This made it easier to stay abstinent.

For me there is no solution, no love, no relief to be found in food. It's never made a bad situation better, only worse, because I only despise myself more for having overeaten.

Every day that I'm abstinent gives me the courage to trust God to get me through one more day. Instead of sleepless nights and worry-filled days, I'm finding serenity. I do what I can for my mother. I've forgiven her for the pain she caused me — and forgiven myself for the pain I've caused her.

I share with other family members how I'm coping with this difficult situation, how using the twelve steps of OA is deepening my trust in God. I see them struggle with their own distress over mom and pray for them, but I know I can't take their hurt away. Neither can I control what happens to them, make them stop eating compulsively, or make them work the twelve steps. They may need this program as much as I do, yet they must decide that for themselves.

But I can find peace with my lack of control. God loves them as much as me. If they should hit bottom, God will be there to help them, too.

As for me, my only choice today is to trust God — and stay abstinent.

Ellisville, Missouri

BACK IN THE GAME

I recently received a phone call informing me that a friend was extremely ill and might not live much longer. This really shook me up because I love my friend very much but had never told him so and, in fact, hadn't talked to him in months.

When I received this news I was practicing my food addiction and initially I ate over it, although I wish I could say I didn't. But then something happened. My Higher Power wouldn't let me isolate myself any longer.

Feeling desperate, I wrote and mailed a letter expressing my love to my friend, something I've wanted to do for a long time. I made direct amends for isolating myself and neglecting our relationship. At the time I didn't know whether he'd still be alive to receive my letter, but I was able to leave this in the hands of my Higher Power.

At that moment, I was given the gift of abstinence. Suddenly I knew that my active disease is what had kept me from really being there in our relationship, and I was finally entirely ready to have God remove this defect of character.

Incidentally my friend did receive my letter. He wrote back, and I went to see him. I cherish the memory of that visit.

I've decided that no matter what, I'm going to choose relationships over food. I've been to two parties since then, and I've been able to remain abstinent, focusing on the people rather than the food.

> I'VE DECIDED THAT NO MATTER WHAT, I'M GOING TO CHOOSE RELATIONSHIPS OVER FOOD.

One of the parties was with some of my spouse's business associates. Although I hardly knew anyone, I still had a good time. Instead of my usual fear, I went to the party with the thought that "these are people I might like to get to know." But there was a time when the very idea of socializing would have been just too scary.

I have several more social gatherings to attend, and I'm praying that God will help me continue to be there for the people instead of the food.

I'm working on my relationship with my spouse as well. It's really scary. But nothing is as scary as the thought that I might again practice my disease, neglect my relationships, but this time, not have a second chance.

Austin, Texas

TAKING MY MEDICINE

My obsession with food began in the high chair. I have vague memories of my mother feeding me as she and my father argued. As the dispute grew more and more heated, and my mother more nervous, she'd start feeding me faster and faster. The message I received from this was that food was the way to deal with everything.

The marriage dissolved a short time later. Unfortunately my compulsion didn't.

I found my way to OA in 1988 after a bout with cancer. The program helped me get my life together and gave me a way to deal with the fear of recurrence by teaching me to live one day at a time. I got abstinent at my first meeting, and in four months I reached goal weight. I felt wonderful.

In retrospect, I see that I'd concentrated on the numbers. I counted every calorie, and weighed and measured myself instead of the food. I used all the tools of recovery but never worked the steps beyond the third. I needed to get back into life and thought being slim would assist the process.

Being thin, however, doesn't necessarily mean being well. Inside I was the same even though my appearance had changed. I found a job after being unemployed for more than a year. Claiming fatigue I stopped going to meetings. Five months later I relapsed, beginning a two-year physical, emotional, and spiritual descent into hell. I denied to myself that I looked any different, even as I was slowly putting all the weight back on, and more.

Twice during that time I attempted to return to the program. Both times I wasn't ready or willing and after a couple of weeks I gave up.

In May of 1991 I hit bottom. I returned to OA, making a commitment to attend a meeting a day for as long as it would take to get abstinent. There was nowhere else to go. It was "do it or die" — literally.

The first week back in OA was exciting, and the feeling of not being out of control was new and liberating. Now that I wasn't eating constantly, my poor stomach could let me know when I was truly hungry. But I was still eating sugar, telling myself I needed to get off it "slowly." After a week of meetings, I had to be honest; it was time to get clean and sober. For me that meant no sugar at all.

> BEING THIN, HOWEVER, DOESN'T NECESSARILY MEAN BEING WELL.

The second and third weeks were difficult. I was abstinent but sick from the withdrawal, tense, angry, nauseated. My sleep was disturbed, and I was tired.

The first time around in OA, abstinence had come so gently and easily. This time it was a struggle. Those two weeks made a definite impression on me. I'd suffered for this abstinence. It wouldn't be so casually thrown away again.

I'd go to meetings feeling ill and wanting to leave, but by meeting's end, the symptoms would stop. I began to understand that meetings truly were my medicine.

> THE FIRST TIME AROUND IN OA, ABSTINENCE HAD COME SO GENTLY AND EASILY. THIS TIME IT WAS A STRUGGLE.

After three weeks of this I thought I was "all set," and I cut down to one meeting a week. I soon became aware that my abstinence was in jeopardy, and went back to attending a meeting a day, eventually settling on a three-meetings-a-week schedule.

Today is my seventieth day of abstinence. I'm a sponsor for the first time, and I'm receiving so much more from my sponsoree than I could ever give. I'm losing weight very slowly and I'm content with that. I no longer own a scale. As I grow stronger and saner each day, the weight will come off.

This time I'm in the program for keeps. I'm so very grateful to be a recovering compulsive overeater.

Fall River, Massachusetts

THE REPRIEVE

I'm a rock-bottom, in-the-gutter type of compulsive eater, now abstinent and recovering by the grace of God. Whenever I speak at a meeting, my sponsor always reminds me beforehand to tell my "I almost died" story. It's important for me to keep the memory green, and also vital to let the people listening to me know exactly how bad things can get.

I won't go into the gory details here. Suffice it to say that I had no less than five life-threatening physical problems when I came back into OA after my relapse, all of which were directly related to compulsive overeating and purging.

When I returned to OA, it took me a while to get abstinent. The sixth attempt was the one that produced lasting abstinence. I think it happened not because I was finally ready and willing at that point, but because the sixth withdrawal nearly finished me off. When I stopped vomiting, fainting, seeing and hearing hallucinations, and feeling suicidally depressed, I had learned one important thing: If I overeat again, it might kill me. I couldn't afford to risk even a slip — it might trigger a fatal relapse.

My first time around in OA, I was one of those people who refused to follow a food plan. At the age of twenty-two, and in a very early stage of my compulsive eating, I didn't need to. But my disease progressed rapidly over the last few years. There are foods which I could eat moderately my first time in OA which I cannot consume safely now. I have to watch my food-related activities and emotions very carefully. I can't afford the occasional slips I had when I was in OA the first time. I need to maintain consistent abstinence in order to survive.

I no longer feel a need to rebel against food planning. Every evening after dinner, I write down what I plan to eat the next day and call it in to my sponsor. I carry it around on a little 3"x 5" card. If something isn't on the plan, I don't eat it. I have learned from painful experience that I cannot make moderate choices about food when I am hungry. I plan my food when I have a full stomach, and I don't deviate from that plan.

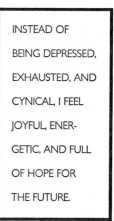

INSTEAD OF BEING DEPRESSED, EXHAUSTED, AND CYNICAL, I FEEL JOYFUL, ENERGETIC, AND FULL OF HOPE FOR THE FUTURE.

I have been cleanly abstinent for 109 glorious days as I write this article. I have lost fifty-one pounds and my physical health is much improved through not carrying that extra weight. My health is excellent. All five life-threatening conditions reversed themselves within the first two months of abstinence. My emotional condition is much better, too. Instead of being depressed, exhausted, and cynical, I feel joyful, energetic, and full of hope for the future.

As I continue to abstain, work the steps, and use the tools of recovery, I realize how badly off I was before I returned to OA. My husband sometimes comments that he is living with a different person. It's a wonder our marriage survived the progression of my illness; I was a bitter, sick, unhappy person for several years.

I'm not trying to suggest that everything is now perfect. My health has not yet completely returned, I occasionally fall prey to exhaustion, and my immune system is still not normal. Every cold or virus that's going around finds me and puts me through the wringer. But I no longer greet each day with a migraine and end it with heart palpitations, wondering whether I will survive another day or even if I want to survive. By the grace of God and the power of the OA program, I have been given the greatest gift of all: a daily reprieve from the deadly illness of compulsive eating. It is worth any amount of effort to maintain that.

Wilmington, Delaware

A GIFT JUST FOR ME

I came to OA in December of 1983. In July of 1990, I celebrated one year of abstinence. For years I prayed for an abstinence I could live with, one where I didn't have to weigh and measure every piece of food, swear off certain foods forever, or feel like a freak at social gatherings and restaurants.

At the end of my long relapse I'd become totally powerless over food and resigned myself to being overweight for the rest of my life. I planned to continue overeating but hoped I would not gain any more weight, and that one day this food and weight thing would straighten itself out.

To be honest I don't know how I got abstinent. I think the God of my understanding looked beyond my faults and saw my needs. Abstinence was a gift from my Higher Power, obtained through working and participating in OA's twelve-step program. The only conscious effort I put forth in dealing with the food was to be honest. For someone as skilled as I am in denial that's not always easy, especially since food is my preferred drug of choice.

My abstinence today consists of three moderate meals a day and sometimes a snack. Aside from the Christmas season, I've not felt deprived or driven to eat to the point of insanity. And this past Christmas, I managed to keep my precious gift of abstinence intact.

I've lost thirty-five pounds. I believe a stricter food plan would have enabled me to lose more weight. When OA still had food plans, I loved the quick weight loss, but found that I couldn't wait to add back certain foods, felt totally nuts until my next meal, and had a "better-than" attitude towards other members who weren't working their food plan the "right" way (*my* way). And I felt like a complete failure when I went off it. This wasn't freedom. This was bondage to a food plan and an example of "stinking thinking."

> TO BE HONEST
> I DON'T KNOW
> HOW I GOT
> ABSTINENT.

Today I trust my life and my food to my Higher Power. Anything that can relieve me of the compulsion to overeat and not make me crazy is something I can turn my life over to. Thank You, God, and thank you, OA.

Los Angeles, California

STEPPING OFF THE SEESAW

My husband and I have moved long distances four times in the past twenty years. With each move, my body "magically" acquired twenty to thirty pounds as I fed my feelings of insecurity. At each new location I would diet off the extra pounds only to see them reappear with the next move.

I became an expert at the weight seesaw. If the Olympics offered a seesaw competition, I'd qualify for team captain. Two years ago I attended my first OA meeting and began working the steps. I found both abstinence and a wonderful sponsor. I lost twenty pounds and gained in self-esteem.

Then the bottom fell out. We both found ourselves without jobs in a depressed area and under a great deal of stress as we tried piecing our lives back together. A business venture didn't work out, and we realized we needed to leave the area in order to earn a living.

> I'VE MANAGED TO LIVE THROUGH THIS WITHOUT GETTING ON THAT SEESAW AGAIN.

The past year has been extremely difficult as we've struggled to sell our house, move on, and start anew. But thanks to my God, the OA program, and the wonderfully supportive people in it, I've managed to live through this without getting on that seesaw again.

Though my abstinence is far from perfect I accept the fact I've made much progress spiritually, emotionally, and physically. Striving for perfection has only gotten me into trouble anyway. Now I'm free to accept myself, rejoice in who I am, and look forward to the joy and challenge of each new day.

Albany, Georgia

IT WORKS IF YOU WORK IT

The disease of compulsive overeating is cunning, baffling, and powerful. It uses any means possible to rob us of our program and recovery, manipulating us into continuing to use excess food for survival. It keeps us in the bondage of food, fat, overeating, and self-obsession. The disease cuts us off from the world and closes the pathway to God.

Our recovery is contingent on the elimination of compulsive overeating from our lives so that we can reopen that pathway and keep it clear. It's only through abstinence that we can do that.

The Twelve Steps and Twelve Traditions of Overeaters Anonymous focuses on freedom from compulsive eating. I believe that this concept encourages us not only to eliminate behaviors such as bingeing, eating certain foods, or eating at certain times and places, but also to eliminate all those behaviors that tend to lead us into compulsive eating, and those that allow us to find comfort in food, be it excess or not.

To those of us who've come a long way emotionally, spiritually, and physically, but who still carry excess weight (of which I am one), I can only say that it's the continuous elimination of compulsive eating behaviors that leads to continued recovery from this disease.

As long as I'm overweight, I'm eating more food than my body needs, and if I'm eating more than I need, I'm overeating. Simple overeating leads to compulsive overeating — which can lead me right out of the program. And some who leave the program never find their way back.

THE DISEASE CUTS US OFF FROM THE WORLD AND CLOSES THE PATHWAY TO GOD.

I have to take my abstinence seriously. Everything else in my life must revolve around it. There's no other road to recovery for me but the one paved with abstinence, and there's no other guidance on that road but my spirituality. The two go hand in hand. I can't have one without the other.

If I remain overweight, then there are still some food choices and eating behaviors that I'm not turning over to God. It means I've not enriched my spiritual life enough to eliminate these things. I must continue to eliminate them if I want continued recovery. No matter where I am in recovery or how much I weigh, I must always be willing to turn over more than I think I need to, especially when it comes to food.

No, thinness doesn't mean wellness — but being overweight doesn't either. I believe I can be free of the compulsion and the fat. There's nothing to fear. God will take me there if I'm willing to give up the crutch of excess food. I have to get out of my own way and let God do the work.

Hickory, North Carolina

IN ALL HONESTY

Today I am a gratefully abstaining compulsive eater recovering one day at a time. How do I know when I've broken my abstinence? My answer is simply, honesty. Abstinence is defined in OA literature as "refraining from compulsive eating." Writing down my food plan daily and committing it to God as I understand God, to myself, and to another human being was how I achieved the very first day of abstinence I ever experienced nearly ten years ago. There are times when I need to make on-the-spot changes and that's when the telephone and prayer and meditation help to keep my focus on my recovery and not my disease. My life today depends, first and foremost, on being abstinent. Working with a sponsor, identifying my personal binge foods, and planning well-balanced, attractive meals help me to plan for an abstinent day.

My food plan has been modified during my ten years in program, but my commitment to abstinence, living and eating guiltfree, using the tools, and living the twelve steps to the best of my ability hasn't changed.

How do I know if I'm abstinent today? By living my life with complete honesty.

Tuckerton, New Jersey

A TOOL, A GIFT, A WAY OF LIFE

Abstinence is something with which I've been struggling for some time. In AA it was an easier issue for me to understand, although not necessarily an easier thing to achieve. "Don't drink and go to meetings," was what I was told in AA and that's what I did. With the help of friends, family, and AA members, I used abstinence as a tool of recovery, a self-imposed abstinence from alcohol, until I could work the twelve-step program enough to become willing to accept abstinence as a gift from my Higher Power.

Being sober for over ten years, I occasionally forget how my gift of abstinence from a "killing compulsion" came about. The freedom from that compulsion did not happen overnight, however, and I did not have a spiritual experience anything like the one Bill W. describes. My compulsion to drink just drifted away after I had been actively working the twelve-step program for about two years.

No specific date, no sudden transformation from a miserable death-row drunk into a spiritually enlightened soul floating forevermore on a sea of serenity. It was just that the compulsion to drink had been removed by my Higher Power — once I became willing to let it go. So simple but so hard to do, and so hard to believe that it would really happen.

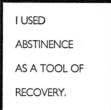

I USED ABSTINENCE AS A TOOL OF RECOVERY.

When I came to OA I wanted my food compulsion to be taken away in the same way as my compulsion to drink. Right now, however, I may not be spiritually ready and willing to let the food compulsion go.

Until I am willing I will continue to use abstinence as a tool of recovery, a self-imposed attempt to refrain from compulsive overeating while totally abstaining from what I honestly know to be my binge foods. It's not unlike the sobriety I practiced as a newly recovering alcoholic, and it should provide some stability in my life until I am willing to let go of my food compulsion and accept God's gift of abstinence as a way of life. I also need to remember that abstinence as a tool of recovery and abstinence as a gift from my Higher Power are not incompatible, but actually a logical progression through the twelve steps of recovery.

How long will that take? A month? A year? Maybe two? The point is that, until it happens, abstinence as a tool of recovery is not just okay, it's necessary until I'm spiritually healthy enough to let my Higher Power take the food compulsion away. Then I'll have abstinence as a way of life.

Daly City, California

WORTHWHILE STRUGGLE

For me, the disease of compulsive overeating began with graze eating and occasional binges. Over the years it progressed to daily binges, midnight raids of the refrigerator, and all the humiliating behaviors that came with trying to satisfy my craving for more — taking food back out of the trash can, gorging myself at salad bars, banquets, and potlucks, and eating with two hands, wishing I had three. But, of course, "more" was never enough.

The evening that I made an unconditional surrender to abstinence and to a Higher Power, I'd felt anything but faith. I was full of food, full of fear, and had only the tiniest hope that I could live free of excess food and correct the unmanageable life that my compulsive overeating had created.

GOD SAW ME THROUGH THE FOOD WITHDRAWALS, GAVE ME THE POWER TO AVOID MY "FIRST BITE," AND LED ME INTO A RICHLY REWARDING NEW LIFE.

During my bingeing days, there were times I could not shut the pantry or refrigerator door for fear of being separated from food. The thought of going from breakfast to lunch, lunch to dinner, and dinner to bedtime without eating in between seemed overwhelming.

Yet I knew I couldn't go on eating and living under the lashes of this progressive and fatal disease. I adopted a three-meal-a-day abstinence, staying away from second helpings, snacks, and binge foods. I asked God to help me keep this commitment under all conditions. I began the withdrawal process that taxed my body, mind, and emotions beyond anything I had ever experienced.

It is painfully clear to me why a return to the disease of compulsive overeating seems an attractive alternative to enduring the initial withdrawal symptoms. Newly abstinent, I recall crying when I'd finished my meals. I wanted more! I watched "normal" folks eat dessert with impunity; why couldn't I? And many nights I lay awake, food calling to me.

Sometimes, when the craving to eat was very strong, I'd take a shower, take a walk, or make a phone call. I knew that the only way out of the disease for me was to avoid the first bite, with God's help. I was, and still am, willing to go to any length to recover.

I often had to turn down the volume on the mental voice that said it was okay to have "just a little" food. I learned to reprogram my thinking through OA literature and meetings. My emotions during that time were strong and varied. Dealing with relationships, work, and daily living became a minute-by-minute challenge.

Why did I endure that anguish when I knew that food could temporarily straighten out my thoughts, feelings, and physical discomfort? Because I wanted to be mentally free, emotionally alive, and physically healthy. I had to believe that these withdrawal symptoms would not last. Hope and faith, if only a little, were my guiding lights.

It's been more than six years since I made my commitment to abstinence. God saw me through the food withdrawals, gave me the power to avoid my "first bite," and led me into a richly rewarding new life. It hasn't been a painfree journey, yet the freedom I feel has been worth every effort. I could not then, nor can I now, make this journey alone. I need each and every one of you to walk with me.

Corona del Mar, California

IT'S A PERSONAL CHOICE

For several years I have wrestled with the question of whether alcohol could be a part of my plan of abstinence from compulsive overeating. I never thought of myself as an alcoholic. I didn't fit my image of an alcoholic; I didn't even like the word. Yes, you could say I abused alcohol, but that occasional abuse seemed like nothing when compared to my daily abuse of food.

Food was always my drug of choice. Destructive relationships came next. Alcohol was not even a close third. So I convinced myself that I could be abstinent and still drink occasionally. I could control it. And, for the most part, I did control it. I cut down substantially on my drinking, reserving it for special occasions.

But even after four years in OA, my abstinence from compulsive overeating never lasted for more than a few months at a time. While I may have thought I was able to handle alcohol, I knew I wasn't able to handle the aftereffects of drinking. I found that when I drink, abstinence from compulsive overeating and from destructive relationships seems much less important.

Can alcohol be a part of my abstinence? I think not. It's not worth the price of my abstinence. Nothing is.

Loudonville, New York

CRUCIAL STEP

I had been in Overeaters Anonymous for almost three years and had lost 130 pounds. My relationship with God was the most important part of my recovery. I truly believed that God was removing my obsession with food.

Then it happened. Relapse. I started gaining a little weight and became consumed by the fear of regaining it all. I expressed this fear to many OA friends. While I will always be grateful for their constant friendship during this trying time, I was unable to accept their help.

The problem was that I had stopped believing in step two, and was totally unwilling to practice step three. During the next three years I gained back all my weight plus a little extra. I felt hopeless but I kept showing up at meetings several times a week. Often I considered not going because I was afraid newcomers would look at me and wonder if the program worked. Even so, I continued to go to meetings because I knew that OA and its principles were my only hope for a better life.

But what was wrong?

Finally someone suggested that I do a spiritual inventory. The seed was planted.

For weeks I considered doing the inventory, but I didn't know how to begin. I summoned the courage to ask the person who'd suggested it if she would recommend some issues I might address. I firmly believe God had placed this precious person in my life.

I followed some of her suggestions and was amazed at the outpouring of conflicts that existed between me and Higher Power. When I gave away my spiritual inventory, I realized that I needed to reevaluate my concept of God and determine what God could and would do for me. Until I took this step, I was unable to believe that a Power greater than myself would restore my abstinence.

> I FELT HOPELESS BUT I KEPT SHOWING UP AT MEETINGS SEVERAL TIMES A WEEK.

It was hard for me to develop my own concept of God, but once I did, I was able to turn over the extra food, the food thoughts, and my fear of dying from compulsive overeating. I have been able to stay abstinent one day at a time for nine weeks. I now want to be abstinent more than I want to overeat. This is truly a miracle from my loving Higher Power, because I was almost certain I would never experience recovery again. But God can and will do for me what I am unable to do for myself as long as I believe God alone has the power.

Leavenworth, Kansas

ABSTINENT AND SMOKE-FREE

At the basis of my disease was an inability to accept myself the way I am — 6'1", left-handed, flat-chested, large-hipped. As the child of an alcoholic, I learned the art of self-loathing early in life. My adolescence was acutely painful; by the age of fifteen, food was my chief comfort and self-derision was my favorite pastime.

I'd always known I was a compulsive overeater. I was also aware that if I drank much at all, I would probably become an alcoholic. So I avoided booze, but I ate instead. I survived to mid-life on the yo-yo cycle of pills and diets, very often depressed.

I began my recovery from compulsive overeating at the same time my alcoholic parent joined AA. I went to OA meetings because I wanted to contribute to the health of my family, not because I was motivated by self-love. During the first year, I continued to overeat (so for a long time I did not count that year as "recovery"), but I gave up my major addictions to destructive relationships and drugs. I got a sponsor and worked the steps. I trained myself to eat only three meals a day and went to every OA meeting I could.

> DURING THE FIRST YEAR, I CONTINUED TO OVEREAT (SO FOR A LONG TIME I DID NOT COUNT THAT YEAR AS "RECOVERY"), BUT I GAVE UP MY MAJOR ADDICTIONS TO DESTRUCTIVE RELATIONSHIPS AND DRUGS.

The second year, I found a very lanky sponsor and tried a food plan she suggested. I shrank to a weight even thinner than what I'd weighed when I was twelve; I felt like a child again. My menstrual cycle ceased for the next three years. I had no idea that anorexia was part of my disease. It was only through the loving confrontations and support of OA friends that I found the courage to let go of my rigidity concerning food.

My years in OA have been ones of personal growth; in them, I have come face-to-face with enormous amounts of fear. It seemed that behind each fear was another, an endless supply of terror that kept me clinging to anything that offered security.

My best friends were my cigarettes. It took me a long, long time to admit that smoking hampered my recovery by masking my feelings. I knew I was still "using" but I was terrified I'd gain weight if I quit. How could I, abstinent so long, quit smoking and risk losing control?

By working the OA program — and with very definite help from my Higher Power who removed my desire for cigarettes — I was able to quit. The miracle is that I only gained about fifteen pounds, which I've read is a typical weight gain experienced by people who quit smoking. At times my abstinence was a two on a scale of one-to-ten, but not once was I drawn to my old ally, sugar.

I can't minimize the experience of quitting smoking; it was awful, terrible at times. But the twelve-step program made it possible. Over and over I said to myself, "Nobody said this would be easy, but it is possible." I grieved my smokes. I cried for no reason. I suffered anxiety attacks. I went to lots of meetings.

In July of last year, I celebrated seven years of abstinence in OA, my fortieth birthday, and one year without cigarettes. I am very happy with myself. This is the reason: I accept myself today just as I am — forty years old, wrinkling, single, a size bigger, and not a bit richer. I love me. What a gift I have given myself. What miracles have come from just three little words — "Keep coming back."

Santa Cruz, California

Four

ABSTINENCE — A PRIORITY

TAKING ACTION

How elusive is abstinence! It darts in and out, scaring the socks off us!

Some people can live with it, but I couldn't until I got a food plan — my very own, designed specifically for my needs — and until working the steps taught me how to live with abstinence.

Other changes in my life have come from working the steps, and I have my sponsor to thank for this. Nancy didn't start out as my sponsor. I never called her or asked her for help. (I had telephone phobia, you understand. I knew how to isolate myself.) She was just a friend in program working her twelfth step who called me one day and asked, "How've you been?" And then she meddled, telling me, "You know, you're never going to get anywhere until you do your fourth step."

Oh, the fourth step. I had abstained from that as well as the food. I realized I had to do it, so I asked Nancy if I could read it to her. In my fifth step, she lived through my long, woeful accounts of who'd done me wrong and where I was to blame, and all the ugliness in my life reared its head. Character defects, I believe they're called. I had yet to learn about those.

Nancy was so gracious. Her eyes only glazed over once while I read. When I finished, she hugged me and told me I was okay. She understood. She knew what I was talking about.

I practice other abstinences as well. I now abstain from jealousy, which used to be my big thing. I'm learning to walk away from pride and let it shrivel up and die! I abstain from worrying, and I'm learning to trust that others can take care of themselves. I refrain from nagging and trying to control other people — I used to major in those. Now I just take one day at a time and live and let live. I wonder where I got that — program, perhaps?

I also stay away from slippery people, places, and things, which for me are drive-throughs, church dinners, and certain family celebrations; yet I've realized abstinence goes deeper than our behavior in a kitchen or at a restaurant. It touches every area of our lives. Abstinence requires a life plan, not simply a food plan. That's why we have the twelve steps. That's why we have a program.

We will never be abstinent from compulsive overeating as long as we talk about it. We will forever sit on the sidelines and long for what others have, feeling flawed and inadequate ourselves. Abstinence is an action. To have what they have, we have to be willing. We have to reach out. We have to accept. We have to find out and do what they did. And if we see someone drowning in our midst, too overwhelmed by life to utter the word "help," we can throw out the lifeline.

Does abstinence come overnight? For some, yes; but for many of us, gaining it is a process. Within the past two years, my mother has died, my father-in-law has had cancer, my brother-in-law has become terminally ill, and we've moved twice. I would have kicked against all this at one time. Now I accept it. I'm taking it one day at a time, one step at a time. I'm finding serenity and — amazingly enough — the ability to refrain from compulsive overeating.

> DOES ABSTINENCE COME OVERNIGHT? FOR SOME, YES; BUT FOR MANY OF US, GAINING IT IS A PROCESS.

Nothing has happened overnight, but it has happened. The key is to keep coming back. It works if you work it. Some of us have to work it a long time. Then one day, as if by magic, something clicks, and we've made it.

We may find we don't have perfect abstinence, but we learn from our humanness and we go on. We learn to think, to act on life rather than react to it, to accept what we can't do anything about, and to change what we can. We can only change our actions, our thought processes, and our patterns of interacting.

Abstinence is my hiding place. Where I once turned to food, I now turn to this safe haven where I take care of myself and entrust my family to the God of my understanding. That's not a bad place to be.

Begin this process by loving yourself. Work the steps with the help of God and a sponsor. You can find abstinence, joy, and peace. That is OA's gift. Receive it! You deserve to be abstinent.

Ocean City, Maryland

ABSTAINING COMES FIRST

I disagree with A *Commitment to Abstinence*'s definition of abstinence. For me, compulsive overeating and bingeing are behaviors caused by a reaction to specific foods. Therefore abstinence is refraining from consuming foods with addictive qualities.

In AA either you're sober or you're not. Members abstain from all alcohol. I can no longer identify myself as a compulsive overeater without recognizing that first and foremost I'm a food addict, addicted to certain foods that cause me to act compulsively in all areas of my life.

I'm no longer confused about differing ideas on abstinence. It has taken me fifteen years to sort out an abstinence of specific addictive foods, and I feel clean and free from addiction today.

Abstinence is the most important thing in my life. If I am eating compulsively — bingeing — every aspect of my life is affected. I no longer have any contact with a spiritual being. I've taken back the job of being my own god. I've given the food the power of being more powerful than God, and there is no longer any rhyme or reason to my life.

I see now that when I wasn't refraining from eating addictive foods, my brain was so fogged I couldn't fully comprehend what the steps meant. I was too busy worrying about where and when I was going to get my next fix to ease the feelings of powerlessness and unmanageability — step one.

I'M NO LONGER CONFUSED ABOUT DIFFERING IDEAS ON ABSTINENCE.

I was looking for food to ease the letting go of dependence on people, places, and things — steps two and three.

I had to have a comforter to relieve the pain of all my character defects and the admission that I was not perfect — steps four and five.

Only God knew how much pain I felt trying to admit, become willing, and having to make amends — steps six, seven, eight, and nine.

I continued to seek food as a god so that I didn't have to take a continuing personal inventory and then admit that I was less than perfect — step ten.

I prayed for the food and to the food, and had no concept of spirituality, only the food — step eleven.

The only message that I could carry to newcomers was that of relapse and irrational thinking because I chose to continue to eat — step twelve.

For me, abstinence must come before working any part of the steps. I don't believe that the steps could make me abstinent. Being willing to feel and learning to deal with life on life's terms came only after I was willing not to pick up the food again. I had to grow up and act like an adult and not a whining child. The tools in conjunction with my abstinence are what have kept me in recovery. I cannot remain abstinent from my compulsive behaviors if I choose to isolate myself by not going to meetings, if I don't ask for help from a sponsor, if I don't set aside time for prayer and meditation, literature, and writing in my journal. And if I don't have a set daily food plan I am not abstinent.

I must protect my own anonymity and that of my fellows. I must continually give back to my fellow members, my group, and my intergroup through service. The tools were designed to insure that I remain abstinent from my addictive foods. But I have to use them. Thank God for OA, my program of recovery, and this wonderful tool of abstinence.

Rockledge, Florida

ABSTINENCE REVISITED

I was in OA the year the food plans were eliminated. My first sponsor made me get on a food plan and then start working the steps. Since then it seems to me that our program focus has shifted away from abstinence.

I understand that abstinence without the steps is just a diet. But there's been a definite shift in our program away from dealing with food. To me, this is a scary proposition. Although we aren't a diet and calorie-counting club, we are Overeaters Anonymous. Our primary purpose is to abstain from compulsive overeating and to share the message of recovery with those who still suffer. We can't separate this program from food; it's both our compulsion and our barometer.

If food is calling, that means something's happening in my life. If I have a problem, and I eat over it, I have two problems. When I'm compulsively overeating I'm unable to focus on anything else.

I know I have another relapse waiting for me if I stop working the steps, using the tools, and practicing the principles of OA's twelve-step program.

There was a time when, in my own mind, I'd become so important to OA that I did every bit of service available. When I

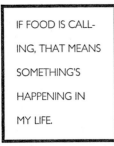

IF FOOD IS CALLING, THAT MEANS SOMETHING'S HAPPENING IN MY LIFE.

moved away from the groups I was serving, I found that I'd been giving service because I thought OA needed me. The truth is that I could have walked out of OA any day, and the Fellowship would still have functioned. People would still have recovered. I was abstaining for OA, not for myself. When I moved away, I relapsed.

From that experience, I learned that I'm a compulsive overeater, and that my disease is progressive and deadly. For me, abstinence is working an eighth and a ninth step on myself — the only way I can make amends to my body for the years of hell I put it through.

Without food as the ruler of my life, I'm free to live and enjoy my newborn baby daughter without the fear that I'll pass on the compulsion to her.

It's not okay for me to compulsively overeat. If I do, I cut myself off from the healing grace of my Higher Power. Without abstinence, I don't have my God, my sanity, or my life. I have to follow the suggestions of this program or I'll die.

I left OA once. That was the most miserable year and a half of my life. I know I can go back to that misery. All I have to do is stop doing what works and try doing things my way again.

I've heard it said that relapse is a part of recovery. I don't believe this. No one has to relapse. Some who do never make it back to the program. That's a chance I'm unwilling to take.

Abstinence is the most important thing in my life without exception. I can't tread the easier, softer way anymore; it'll kill me.

No one ever told me that the road to recovery was easy — but it's easier than compulsive overeating. This disease exists on three levels—spiritual, emotional, and physical. We can't separate them, nor can we work on one aspect without working on the others.

Westmont, Illinois

A PIVOTAL DECISION

I am celebrating nine years of abstinence. For someone who couldn't stay on a diet for longer than three days, that's a miracle — a miracle made possible by OA.

Nine years ago I'd been in OA for four years and had seldom had more than a few days of abstinence. I looked at those who had been abstinent for years and concluded they must not have the same disease.

In those four years I couldn't make much headway with the steps because I didn't have a firm foundation of step one on which to build my recovery. Driven by fear, desperation, and borrowed hope, however, I did learn to use the tools. I got over my fear of making calls, even to those with long-term abstinence. I performed service by setting up chairs and laying out literature at meetings. I formed small relapse recovery groups in my home. I wrote. I meditated. I read program literature.

Since childhood, fear had led me to a strict self-reliance. Only from the agony of compulsive overeating was I propelled to reach out to others for help. After four years in OA I had enough despair and enough hope to surrender completely. I had admitted powerlessness before but not that my life was totally unmanageable. After a week of abstinence I wrote a fourth-step inventory and read it to a friend who had six years of abstinence.

I wavered back and forth on the way home. If I wanted what my friend had — long-term abstinence, clarity, self-respect, recovery — I had to commit 100 percent to abstinence. But what about the "freedom" of eating what and when I wanted? I had a choice: discipline and recovery or "freedom" and sickness. My Higher Power intervened. I made the decision for abstinence.

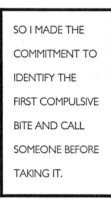

SO I MADE THE COMMITMENT TO IDENTIFY THE FIRST COMPULSIVE BITE AND CALL SOMEONE BEFORE TAKING IT.

But how? After four years of trying and failing, what could I do differently? How could I be sure I would never again, one day at a time, slip back into compulsive overeating? Many times I'd read the OA pamphlet *Before You Take That First Compulsive Bite, Remember* . . . and agreed with it completely. Yet time and time again I ended up back in the food. Why? Because I didn't always know what the first compulsive bite was. Only occasionally did I dive right into a binge, usually I slid there.

So I made the commitment to identify the first compulsive bite and call someone before taking it. Nine years of abstinence began with a single meal. I am no nearer to overeating today than I was nine years ago, and no further either — I'm still just one bite away.

Nine years of practice, commitment, and working the steps have kept me from taking that bite. I turned my food over to a sponsor for the first few years. I couldn't avoid all the binge foods as I'd binged on practically everything, but I did avoid my main ones. I could then fully work the steps, confident that the pain, fear, anger, and joy would not send me back to food. I got honest and clear about what I was eating. I could then learn to be honest about everything else.

A lot has changed in nine years. I eat all kinds of foods now with no cravings, obsession, or compulsion to overeat — I don't plan my meals in advance or commit them to someone unless I'm under great stress and find it comforting to do so. One thing has not changed, however. Whether I'm eating at home, a picnic, a buffet, a restaurant, or a friend's house, I always make the decision as to what the first compulsive bite would be, and commit to make a call before taking it.

My life is wonderful today. I am engaged to be married. I am about to go back to school. The promises have come true for me. It all began with abstinence and my decision to recognize and call before that first compulsive bite nine years ago.

Glorieta, New Mexico

THE ABSTINENCE ADVANTAGE

Abstinence is the most important thing in my life today without exception. It hasn't always been. I've maintained a 65-pound weight loss since coming to OA three and a half years ago, in spite of many ups and downs with abstinence. Recently I was once again humbled by my addiction to food, especially sweets. I now know that no matter what does — or doesn't — happen, today will be a success if I remain abstinent. I can say that because I realize more than ever that only when I am abstinent and free from my overwhelming obsession with food am I able to put other things in my life in perspective. When my focus is on food, everything else is out of focus. I used to cringe when I heard people say that abstinence was the most important thing in their lives. More important than God? I thought that was blasphemy. Now I realize that unless I am abstinent, I can't put God first. When I'm overeating, food becomes my god. I worship it and trust it to make things better. When I am abstinent, I put my trust in God and I'm free to live the rich, full life God has in mind for me.

Sometimes, however, I still forget why it is so important for me to abstain from sweets and from overeating. I've spent the last three and a half years since coming into OA experimenting with various eating plans in an effort to define my own personal abstinence. I've proven over and over, beyond a shadow of a doubt, that when I eat sweets my obsession with food returns and my compulsion takes over my whole life. Even though I know I can be free from the misery that accompanies my obsession simply by abstaining, I still find myself rationalizing and trying to justify eating "just this one sweet thing." Why? Because at least where food is concerned, I'm not sane.

A major symptom or characteristic of my disease is recurring episodes of insanity. During these attacks I forget the pain and misery of compulsive overeating and lose sight of the reasons for abstinence. Abstinence suddenly seems silly, or impossible, or overrated! I think, "What's the big deal about abstinence?" Later, of course, after I've given in to the urge to overeat, my sanity returns, and I realize the price I have paid for once again having given in to my disease.

> A MAJOR SYMPTOM OR CHARACTERISTIC OF MY DISEASE IS RECURRING EPISODES OF INSANITY.

Knowing that I am subject to insanity regarding food, I am learning to talk myself through these situations. I tell myself: "Right now abstinence doesn't seem very important, but that's because of the insanity. I have temporarily forgotten I am a compulsive overeater and have lost sight of the reality of my disease."

But somewhere inside me a tiny, soft-spoken voice (the sane part of me) assures me that remaining abstinent really is the most important thing I can do today. Maybe I don't feel like abstinence is very important at that moment, but it is essential that I remember that feelings cannot always be trusted. I must listen to the little voice of sanity, however weak it may be. I must trust that, in time, the insanity will pass, and I will once again remember why abstinence is so vital.

Now that I'm more aware of the nature of my insanity, perhaps I can learn to recognize the early warning signs before the episodes become full-blown. Maybe I can better recognize the distorted thinking that accompanies these attacks. And maybe it will become easier for me to listen to the quiet voice inside of me. Perhaps the voice will become stronger each time I listen to it.

This disease will be with me all my life and I presume I will always be subject to these recurring episodes of insanity. But there is a method of treatment. The Big Book tells me the good news: There is a solution. There is a way of living which allows me to have a daily reprieve from my illness, as long as I work the steps and am willing to do whatever it takes to have recovery.

Sylacauga, Alabama

ABSTINENCE — IT'S NOT A NUMBERS GAME

L ast night during pitch time I said my piece. But I left the meeting wondering if what I said was what I meant to say. My heart was going out to newcomers and others who have not quite been able to "let go and let God" help them with their abstinence.

Because many OAs in my area are blessed with great gifts of long-standing abstinence, our meetings are often abstinence-oriented. This is a wonderful thing for us, and exactly what I need.

But I have noticed that some of our newcomers and a few of our diligent but nonabstinent members are either dropping out or fighting their reluctance to attend meetings. Because they are not currently abstinent, they are feeling "less than" others.

OA is not a diet club, but it's not an abstinence-seniority club either. OA is a program that uses the twelve steps to help compulsive overeaters find peace, health, and recovery from their food obsession. The first day of abstinence for a newcomer is just as important as day 2,347 for an oldtimer.

Often I begin my pitch with, "Hi! I'm C.W., and I'm a compulsive overeater, and this is my _____ day/month/year of abstinence." For me, my abstinence is something to celebrate. But, thinking back, perhaps I've been a little smug. As I have remained abstinent through the generosity of my H.P., I have gained more compassion for those still compulsively overeating. I have noticed smiles freeze on faces and eyes show despair every time a member proclaims his or her length of abstinence.

So, after much deliberation, I've decided to change my little introduction. From now on I'll say, "Hi, I'm C.W., and I'm a compulsive overeater, and thanks to my H.P., *today* I am abstinent." When they pass around the sheet that lists abstinence birthdays, I won't add my name.

Still, I wonder about what I said last night. I do have a tendency to sound preachy; I'd like to fix everyone and everything — anything to distract me from my problems. Although I have definite opinions about the competition that can result when comparing one member's length of abstinence to another's, I have an even stronger conviction about the concept of abstinence. Before my commitment to abstinence in OA, I allowed greed, self-centeredness, jealousy, and envy to consume me. I was miserable, and I made sure that those closest to me knew it. On the other hand, in my public life I was cheerful and witty, and I would often go out of my way for those who would give me approval or attention. I was at the mercy of my disease for 32 years; I don't want to go back.

Abstinence is absolutely essential to peace and sanity. It is more important than anything to me — more than my religious beliefs and more than my love for my husband, children, and family. And they are all worth going to any length for! You see, if I am not abstinent, I cannot appreciate or participate in those wonders. Abstinent for today, I see with new eyes a world I occupied all my life but never saw; a child's struggles, a husband's disappointment, a beautiful landscape. Abstinent for today, I am willing to go to a movie or a play without the promise that I'll be taken out for a huge dinner also. Abstinent for today, I find that my children are for loving, hugging, fussing over, and holding hands with: not for showering with the tons of sugared treats I bought for them but ate by myself instead.

So, if you were at that meeting and I left you a little confused, I apologize. In the future you won't find me listing my abstinence in number of days. But don't let that fool you — it's still the most important thing in my life.

Aloha, Oregon

KEEP IT SIMPLE

Tradition five states, "Each group has but one primary purpose — to carry its message to the compulsive overeater who still suffers." What is the message? It is the message of abstinence, and the possibility of recovery from the ravages of compulsive overeating.

As it says in the OA preamble, OA is not a diet and calories club. Nor is it group therapy, Al-Anon, ACA, or any other twelve-step Fellowship. OA is the only group that addresses the needs of compulsive overeaters and the possibility of a daily reprieve from compulsive overeating. That is the message I feel needs to be shared in OA meetings.

As the AA Twelve and Twelve states in reference to the fifth tradition, "better do one thing supremely well than many badly. That is the central theme of this tradition." The longer I abstain, which is nine-plus years, the greater is my need to hear stories of recovery from compulsive overeating. Often, however, I hear people pitch about other Fellowships, non-Conference-approved literature, therapy, etc. I know I cannot control what is said in meetings, but I hope OA will come of age in this regard. My life depends on it. Still, I know that I must release the anger I feel about this matter. These days, I'm much more sensitive to it than I used to be, perhaps because I was once as guilty as the next member of not honoring tradition five.

Tradition one is just as important: "Our common welfare should come first; personal recovery depends upon OA unity." In unity there is recovery. Self-indulgence of my own needs, whims, and desires turned me into a 'round-the-clock binger and starver. In my experience, it is abstinence — and abstinence alone — that gives me the opportunity and the clarity to root out the defects that led to my overeating. The only way I can make progress is to put the group's needs ahead of my own, and to carry the message of abstinence to others.

Los Angeles, California

HANDLE WITH CARE

I finally made it — thirty days of abstinence!

I have had several weeks of abstinence a number of times, but I usually broke it about the twenty-fifth or twenty-sixth day. I always sabotaged myself in some way as I neared the "magical" thirty-day mark. Now that that day has come and gone, I realize there is nothing magical about thirty days per se; but there is something miraculous about every day of abstinence.

As I neared the thirty-day mark this most recent time, I saw how poorly I had been treating my very fragile abstinence. I was handling it carelessly, playing with it, almost daring myself to break it. This was most apparent to me during the celebration of a recent holiday.

As part of my personal plan, I chose to refrain from the traditional binge foods that had always represented joy and celebration, and replaced them with good, wholesome foods that my entire family could enjoy. To establish a festive feeling, I prepared the table with the best of everything — fancy place mats, our best china, crystal goblets (not used since our wedding), and a crystal candle holder at each setting.

The only thing "out of place," so to speak, was a cheaper, smaller glass goblet that I set before my six-year-old daughter. I felt I couldn't quite trust her to handle a large crystal goblet. She cried when she saw that she had a different glass, until she noticed that it, too, was fancy and delicate.

As she handled the smaller goblet, I felt my heart leap into my throat several times. She treated it so roughly, pretending to be toasting with everyone, hitting the glass against every available surface, and setting it down a bit too hard after every gulp.

Suddenly, I saw myself in her. I had been handling my abstinence roughly also. As I'd seen the thirty-day mark approach, I was so sure that I would break my abstinence again that I toyed with it. I let myself taste things that I had no business tasting. I wasn't caring for my abstinence lovingly or carefully. Instead, I banged it against every tantalizing situation. No, I never really broke my abstinence — just as my daughter never really broke the goblet but I had many close calls.

And you know, I could tell that my Higher Power was standing near me, guarding the abstinence so graciously given to me. God reached out to catch me whenever I risked falling, just as I had kept a careful eye on my daughter.

My abstinence is so very delicate. I know now that even though I have passed the once-elusive thirty-day mark, I must treat my abstinence with tender loving care and gentleness lest it be broken.

South Jacksonville, Illinois

Five

ABSTINENCE AND THE TOOLS

RETOOLING FOR RECOVERY

I've always used the tools of recovery to a certain degree — done service, had a sponsor, made phone calls, and read the literature. But I never really considered how important all the tools were — and how I could use them to my greatest benefit. Since my return from relapse, I've been learning to use the tools regularly because I never want to go "out there" again.

Abstinence. I define my abstinence as simply not overeating. I try to keep in mind that abstinence is just a tool; the ultimate goal is recovery. This is one of the ways in which abstinence differs from a diet. Abstinence helps me accomplish a total change in lifestyle and character so that I can live a saner and happier life.

I try not to worry too much about other people's food plans. I can get so caught up in the diet mentality that I forget that abstinence means I don't have to worry about whether or not I need to eat more salad!

> I STILL MAKE AS MANY CALLS AS I CAN, OFTEN SPENDING PART OF MY LUNCH HOUR ON THE PHONE WITH THESE DAYTIME FRIENDS.

Sponsorship. It took me several years to get serious about having a sponsor. Even when I found somebody I liked, I called only in emergencies. Then one day my sponsor's sponsor was called out of town, and we agreed to sponsor each other until she returned. We took turns calling one another every day, and my serenity and abstinence improved. Even after her sponsor returned home, I continued calling regularly. I now believe, as one of my OA friends always says, that "Sponsorship is a lifeline to the program."

Meetings. I attend two OA meetings a week. Sometimes I feel a little guilty about this — some of my friends go to meetings nearly every day. I juggle a full-time job and a career as a free-lance writer, but I've made a commitment to fit two meetings into my schedule every week, no matter what. I've heard it said that if we can't have perfect abstinence, we can at least have perfect attendance.

I try to come early and leave late. Taking time to attend a meeting is one of the most important things I can do for myself. Another is putting aside all the other worries and concerns of the day so that I can concentrate on what's being said.

Telephone. Right after my return to OA, my boss went away on vacation leaving me with almost nothing to do. I soon realized I was fixating on the cafeteria and candy machines. I decided to call OA friends during the day. I enjoyed talking to members I'd never come to know very well because they were only available for phone calls during my usual working hours.

I soon built a list of people whom I felt comfortable calling. I still make as many calls as I can, often spending part of my lunch hour on the phone with these daytime friends.

LISTENING TO MYSELF, I SUDDENLY UNDERSTOOD THAT OA WRITING IS ABOUT HONESTY, NOT TALENT OR TECHNIQUE.

Writing. Because I'm a professional writer, I was reluctant to use writing as an aid to recovery. I've heard people in meetings say that they struggled to get their thoughts on paper, but the struggle helped them understand themselves better.

I've been blessed with a total lack of writer's block. I can produce a competent article in a few minutes if there is a tight deadline. Writing was too easy, I thought; it couldn't possibly help me.

I happened to attend a concert during which the performer said something that really made me angry. I discussed it with my sponsor who said, "Why not write a letter and tell him about it?" My immediate response was: "How should I slant the letter? Toward his politics, his belief system, his personal life?"

Listening to myself, I suddenly understood that OA writing is about honesty, not talent or technique. I wrote the letter, deleted it from my computer without printing it, and felt much better!

Literature. I serve as literature secretary for both of my groups. I enjoy leafing through the OA catalog and especially enjoy sharing *Lifeline* with newcomers. I try to keep the groups' *Lifeline* lending libraries up to date by purchasing back issues from the WSO and asking members to bring in their copies after they've read them.

Often I've heard a newcomer say: "I read the pamphlets, but I couldn't understand them very well. Then I read the copy of *Lifeline* you gave me, and I could really relate to the stories in there. That's what made me want to come back."

Anonymity. A couple of years ago, there was a serious anonymity break in our area when a reporter published something he'd heard a local political activist say at an OA meeting. It really frightened me, because as a writer I knew the temptation that reporter felt, and as a politically active person myself, I wondered if I'd be next.

The incident taught us all a lesson about the purpose of anonymity. Our program is a catalyst for the transformation of character. Shedding our hard outer shells and becoming vulnerable are vital to recovery, and we need to know that we can do that in absolute safety.

> THE INCIDENT TAUGHT US ALL A LESSON ABOUT THE PURPOSE OF ANONYMITY. OUR PROGRAM IS A CATALYST FOR THE TRANSFORMATION OF CHARACTER.

Service. Because my schedule is so irregular and hectic, I have to limit my service to things I can do in a spare moment: copying meeting lists, ordering literature, calling newcomers midway through the week. Knowing that I'm on my way to the copy store or the post office to pick up a literature order keeps me from overeating while I'm doing these errands.

I hope this article doesn't sound too boastful. I played the role of "Miss OA" my first time around, and it got me into a lot of trouble! I use the tools not because I "should," but because they work. And if one of them becomes too tiring, I let it go for a while. For instance, some days I just can't fit in any telephone calls. I know people who commit to making a certain number of phone calls every day, but that's not possible for me.

I try to keep in mind that these are the tools of recovery, and

I use them because recovery is my heart's deepest desire. It's a pleasure to be home in OA again.

Wilmington, Delaware

THE PEN IS MIGHTIER THAN THE RELAPSE

This morning I find myself at the point where things usually start to go wrong. Following a two-week abstinence and some progress on the scale, I eat a light and abstinent breakfast, and I'm suddenly filled with rebellion and rage. I want to eat! I want to eat more! — for no reason at all.

I'm not really hungry, yet I'm dying to put something in my mouth. At the same time I'm scared, wanting very much to stay abstinent. And I have a strong desire to write.

I sit quietly, take a few deep breaths, and make some tea. As I slowly sip it, I begin writing. I'm holding on now and starting to relax.

I seem to have weathered the storm. I'm calmer, more at peace, feeling better mentally, physically, and spiritually. I'm actually less hungry.

> I SEEM TO HAVE WEATHERED THE STORM. I'M CALMER, MORE AT PEACE, FEELING BETTER MENTALLY, PHYSICALLY, AND SPIRITUALLY.

This is a miracle! Still writing, I get the idea of sending this to *Lifeline*. Now I'm feeling humble and infinitely grateful. Thank you, OA!

In trying to understand what just happened, I'm very aware of a great deal of pain connected with the idea of "falling off" my abstinence. I had felt something pushing me on to that precipice with a great deal of force. I still don't understand why it happened, but I'm relieved and grateful for how it turned out.

Writing was my rescuer. One more time, I realized why this is my favorite tool. It's always available, is most accommodating to me and my moods, and provides an excellent record for later perusal — and for reference if a similar crisis strikes in the future. In times of stress I find it easier to write than to dial a phone number.

I'm feeling a hundred percent better now, and I've overcome my desire to jump off my abstinence.

Next, I need to take some effective and constructive action. Typing up the story and hopping on my bicycle to mail it to *Lifeline* will be therapeutic — another phase of my healing.

Thank you, Higher Power, thank you, OA, and thank you, *Lifeline*.

Palo Alto, California

SERENITY IN A SUITCASE

I've traveled quite a bit during the eight years of my OA recovery. At first I couldn't go anywhere without being into the food. But in the last five years I've been given the gift of abstinence on business trips, in the mountains, at the beach, and while visiting family.

Away from home I chose not to make meetings a part of my program. I'd pack my daily meditation books, my journal, my phone book, some weighed and measured food — and my Higher Power. I'd keep in touch with my sponsor and OA friends, read program literature, write in my journal, and abstain.

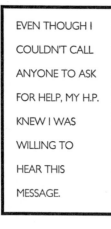

EVEN THOUGH I COULDN'T CALL ANYONE TO ASK FOR HELP, MY H.P. KNEW I WAS WILLING TO HEAR THIS MESSAGE.

This past winter my husband and I flew to Florida for our yearly visit to my parents. The weather was beautiful, so we retreated on a mini-vacation by ourselves. When we returned to finish our stay with my parents, the pain of my childhood of compulsive eating reared its ugly head.

I was surrounded by lots of food not on my food plan, tireless attention to what I was and wasn't eating, and constant banter about food. What a reminder of the way I lived before recovery!

During those two days I was unable to pick up the phone. It was as though I was trapped in the past. One night I thought: "Okay, I've had enough of this pain, I'm going to eat — things I haven't eaten in six years and lots of them!" I just didn't care anymore.

But my H.P. took over. As if being led by the hand, I did what's always worked for me during times of intense stress when the food is calling to me: I read program literature and started writing. This story is a result. I had to share the miracle of abstinence. Even though I couldn't call anyone to ask for help, my H.P. knew I was willing to hear this message.

My H.P. is always there for me; I just need to listen. As I wrote, I heard the voices of my OA friends, just as if I'd called them, telling me how excess food won't make the pain go away. And the teddy bear I got at the 1992 World Service Convention in Baltimore was sitting on the bed right behind me sending me more messages of abstinence!

In twelve more hours I'll be on a plane back to my OA family. This trip reminded me that I need to take all the tools of the OA program with me when I travel. It helped me see that one hour in a meeting away from home can add one more day of serenity and abstinence to my life.

Rockville, Maryland

> IN TWELVE MORE HOURS I'LL BE ON A PLANE BACK TO MY OA FAMILY. THIS TRIP REMINDED ME THAT I NEED TO TAKE ALL THE TOOLS OF THE OA PROGRAM WITH ME WHEN I TRAVEL.

TAMING THE BEAR

I recently read an account of a fatal bear attack. It was a sad story, but not one which would usually keep me awake at night. But it did. I was struck by how ill-prepared was the victim, and how irrational and persistent the bear.

I'm in my fifth year of program and actively working the steps to the best of my ability, faithfully attending meetings and sponsoring as well. Lately though my abstinence hasn't been all I want it to be; thoughts of food and bingeing have become more frequent and compelling.

I couldn't put the bear attack out of my mind. I talked it over with an OA friend and discovered I identified with the victim. I felt like a silent witness as she stood alone — helpless, hopeless, unarmed, and defenseless. I can imagine what horror filled her mind in her last moments because, in some measure, I know.

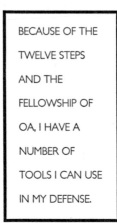

BECAUSE OF THE TWELVE STEPS AND THE FELLOWSHIP OF OA, I HAVE A NUMBER OF TOOLS I CAN USE IN MY DEFENSE.

I am that woman, and the bear is my disease. It, too, is irrational. It has nothing to gain from my death, yet it singlemindedly seeks to consume me.

Unlike that unfortunate woman, however, I am not alone and helpless. Because of the twelve steps and the Fellowship of OA, I have a number of tools I can use in my defense.

Strongest of these is my Higher Power, always available and only a prayer away. I have my sponsor and my fellow OAs. I have meetings for support, literature for information and inspiration, writing for release and understanding, the telephone and service to get me out of myself.

I can choose to go alone into the wilderness or I can go prepared.

Milton, Washington

SHARING THANKS

Thank God I compulsively purchased all the OA literature seven years ago after I returned to OA following a painful three-year relapse. I've been disheartened about OA lately, constantly comparing it to my "old" meetings and finding the new meetings wanting. I moved from Boston to a little town where food-plan meetings are all the rage and step meetings are scarce.

Early this morning I was melancholy and missing my old, more spiritual meetings. I picked up my *Lifeline Sampler* and read "Visit to a Small Meeting." It's a beautiful story, full of gratitude and abstinence, about a member who is a one-person meeting. It made me realize I should be grateful for my situation. There are step meetings without food requirements in this area, attended by people with my kind of spiritual life.

But I still miss my Boston meetings. I sat in the same seats three times a week for four years. It will take me a long time to find three comfortable seats here. I miss that gloriously joyous feeling that comes from sharing and hearing others share their practice of the twelve steps. Yet I am confident that feeling will return.

I'm grateful to everyone who ever shared at an OA meeting. Your quest for abstinence and serenity, your sharing and your dumping, your anger and your joy have taught me to live a life without compulsive overeating. I have just celebrated seven years of abstinence. Together we did what I couldn't do alone.

Tewksbury, Massachusetts

> YOUR QUEST FOR ABSTINENCE AND SERENITY, YOUR SHARING AND YOUR DUMPING, YOUR ANGER AND YOUR JOY HAVE TAUGHT ME TO LIVE A LIFE WITHOUT COMPULSIVE OVEREATING.

Six

ABSTINENT LIVING

AN ABSTINENT VACATION

Our vacation of a lifetime had been in the works for nearly six months, well before I was introduced to OA. Now, only two months abstinent, I was preparing to leave on a week-long adventure aboard a sixty-five foot sailboat in the Bahamas. We were planning to enjoy a week of scuba diving and sailing — no phones, no TV, no alarm clocks. I was faced with a week of being out in the middle of the ocean with very limited food options.

> I KNOW THAT I CAN DEAL WITH MY FEELINGS TODAY WITHOUT SHOVING SOMETHING IN MY MOUTH.

Determined to stick to my food program, I called the cruise office to discuss my needs. I was assured that special consideration would be extended, and there would be no problem. I called again a few days later to hear a similar reassurance.

The week before we left, I attended every available OA meeting. While taking every precaution, I was acutely aware of how cunning, baffling, and powerful my disease is. To be stranded in the middle of nowhere with minimal food choices was frightening.

Finally the big day arrived. I was armed with my measuring cups, scales, and scads of literature, including, of course, a few copies of *Lifeline*. But as we drove to the port in Miami, I couldn't dismiss my fear. I used the biggest tool available to me: I prayed. As I talked with my Higher Power and "let it go," I felt calmer and knew that somehow everything would be all right.

Once on board I stopped the first crew member I found and asked to be directed to the galley. I explained that I was the passenger who would be the pain in the neck concerning meals.

"Don't worry about anything," he said with a soft smile. "The cook puts up with me, and I'm a recovering alcoholic." I couldn't believe my ears. He introduced me to the cook who confided she, too, was in recovery in another twelve-step program.

What a vacation this turned out to be! I explained my food

program to the cook, and she weighed, measured, and served every one of my meals. Total abstinence! We found one more friend of Bill W. and the four of us watched the sun rise every morning, sipping coffee and sharing in a very casual twelve-step meeting.

I know that I can deal with my feelings today without shoving something in my mouth. One day at a time at home, work, or even on vacation, I have my Higher Power, the tools, and the twelve steps to help me live my life. I celebrated ninety days of abstinence last week.

Orlando, Florida

A FITTING ORGANIZATION

I got out of bed and pulled on a freshly laundered pair of jeans. I buttoned the top and zipped them up without violently contorting myself and dancing around the room. This was nothing short of a miracle!

Several weeks ago the project team I'm on at work was informed that its members would have to work six-day weeks, in addition to overtime, Monday through Friday. The future of the company, we were told, depended upon us finishing the project and delivering it to our customer. As the senior member of the team my manager let me know that I was expected to be a shining example — arrive early and stay late.

Before OA I handled this kind of stress by eating. I'd begin by wolfing down a greasy fast-food breakfast in rush-hour traffic, followed by a mid-morning, junk-food snack. After an equally greasy lunch at my desk, I'd have two or three more snacks. My little free time in the evening would be spent grazing in the fridge and the cupboards. I'd tell myself I needed all the food "to keep up my energy," while I stuffed down my anger, frustration, and resentment. By the end of each

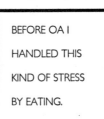

BEFORE OA I

HANDLED THIS

KIND OF STRESS

BY EATING.

project I'd have gained at least twenty pounds.

But now, thanks to daily contact with a Higher Power and the tools I've learned through OA, I am able to maintain an abstinence which allows me to keep my weight stable despite the stress. Even more important I'm learning to practice these principles in all my affairs. I've made clear to my supervisor that I have to take care of my needs first, especially making time for OA meetings and for rest. I've stated what I will do and how I am willing to work, disregarding my supervisor's unrealistic expectations instead of letting them drive me crazy. I lead my team by example, showing how to break down the problem into manageable pieces and work through them in an organized fashion from beginning to end. My team's aim will be progress, not perfection. I'm learning to let go of the results, trusting things to happen in H.P.'s time instead of mine.

The project will be ready for our customers when each team member has completed his or her task. The result will be satisfactory because we will have followed directions for building in quality, instead of slapping things together in a panic and hoping no one notices. The team members will not be burned out from stress. We can be proud of what we've accomplished and will be ready to tackle the next project with tools to better manage our time and its needs. But most important to me, my jeans will still fit. Thanks to OA.

Fremont, California

SWEET SURRENDER

There I was, sober and abstinent for three years, back to normal in body weight, involved with daily meetings in South Bend, working closely with my sponsor, and depending on all the tools for sanity. Then my boss offered me a six-week job checking transmission lines in northwestern Pennsylvania. A new truck, video equipment, and a computer would help me cover fifteen miles of line daily. Sounded almost like a vacation.

But on the first day I was shocked to discover I would have to hike twelve to fourteen miles over rugged terrain just to cover a measly six miles of line in one day, Monday through Saturday. To inspect 490 miles of power lines would take four months, through fall and early winter.

The job was impossible. I couldn't possibly finish it. Would I break a leg in the middle of a forest? Be shot by drunken hunters? Mauled by wild dogs? Drowned in a swamp?

Worst of all none of the towns I stayed in was larger than Mishawaka, Indiana, and few people had even heard of OA.

I missed breakfast the first day because my boss refused to stop before reaching the site. I hiked four miles across rivers, fields, and pastures before sitting down to lunch at a greasy diner in Conneautville.

I was hungry. But, by the grace of God, I didn't binge. I ate an abstinent lunch. I didn't allow the circumstances to become an excuse for bingeing.

For two weeks I lost weight and starved between meals. I ate bigger portions but nothing inappropriate. I didn't crave my binge foods. One night I finished a big dinner in Meadville and felt like vomiting. Choking back tears, I headed for the phone in the lobby. Thank God my sponsor was home. I felt I had binged, even though I hadn't. "I want to cut my food intake," I cried.

> I WAS HUNGRY. BUT, BY THE GRACE OF GOD, I DIDN'T BINGE. I ATE AN ABSTINENT LUNCH. I DIDN'T ALLOW THE CIRCUMSTANCES TO BECOME AN EXCUSE FOR BINGEING.

"If you cut down you'll set yourself up for a real binge," my sponsor replied. "Your body needs the fuel, but your stomach is too small to stoke the furnace. Go slow, don't skip, pray, and get to a meeting."

I discovered how the steps and tools can help me no matter where I am. The area had many strong AA meetings where I met new friends, even some OAs. Calling my recovery friends back home helped so much, too. I pored over my emergency stack of *Lifelines* whenever I felt vulnerable to insanity and isolation.

I learned how to zoom through forests, navigate around and through swamps, jump electric and barbed wire fences, climb Allegheny mountain trails and crisscross timber, oil, and corn country. I had no partner so I had to hike down-line for a mile or two and backtrack to the truck alone.

Soon I noticed that my meals were all consistent. Body weight and size returned to normal and stayed constant. I felt healthy and energetic. All of this without trying to manage the food. A miraculous truce with food followed me every step of the way.

> A MIRACULOUS TRUCE WITH FOOD FOLLOWED ME EVERY STEP OF THE WAY.

The real crisis was accepting my job and my life in Pennsylvania. Would I finish? Would the boss crucify me for mistakes? Would I break the $3,000 equipment they made me haul cross-country? When would I fall in love and live happily ever after?

I found a meeting in Meadville and a member talked to me afterwards. "Sounds like you're fighting the program. You're making meetings, calls, inventories, prayers, and all that, but you're not letting go. Are you having fun yet?"

"Fun?" I stared at him like an idiot.

"Yes, fun. If you don't turn it over and surrender all your problems to God, how long do you expect to remain sober?"

My first surrender in a long time occurred soon after. I was hiking through a lowland woods in the pouring rain. Switches whipped my face as I struggled through dense, thorny brush. I had to videotape a tower for the second time, and I was angry. I have three degrees, talent, ambition, and ability. Why was I trudging through the woods counting poles?

Then the Serenity Prayer came to mind, and for once I asked God to help. I said aloud the things I had trouble accepting: cold rain, soaked boots, the woods, a crazy job, and loneliness. Could I accept all these for one morning? An enormous burden fell from my shoulders. I felt at peace with myself. Finishing my task in harmony with the way things were became a joy.

For the rest of that day anxiety, obsession, and depression didn't take hold. Food and alcohol held all the appeal of rat poison to me. Every day left on the job I surrendered. When I finally returned home, my portion sizes returned to normal. With God's help, impossible conditions became possible, one day at a time.

South Bend, Indiana

MOVING AHEAD

After eleven years of abstinence, I'd like to share with the readers of *Lifeline* a few insights I have learned on this journey of recovery.

- The food was just a symptom of a deeper problem and served as a "cover-up" for my inner turmoil. With the food in its proper perspective, I must continually work on myself.
- I have feelings. They come and go and are constantly changing. I don't need to do anything about them — I just need to allow them to be. I don't need to let them control my behavior. Being in a bad mood doesn't mean I can be crabby to others.
- This is a twenty-four-hour-a-day program. I need to be on guard for negative thoughts, fear, selfishness, and self-pity. I need to pray for their removal and forgive myself when I indulge in them.
- Constant work on my self-esteem is the key to long-term recovery. Self-hatred kept me in my disease. If I love myself, love others, and love God, I will be more willing to go to any length for freedom from the food compulsion.
- No matter how many days of abstinence I rack up, I still need to share what's going on in my life with my sponsor and other OA friends. Just listening to others and sitting without speaking at meetings won't keep me well. I must

THE FOOD WAS JUST A SYMPTOM OF A DEEPER PROBLEM AND SERVED AS A "COVER-UP" FOR MY INNER TURMOIL.

open my heart.

- It's very important that I work on being on good terms with others. Hatred, resentment, and judgment hurt only me. The only way to be free from those emotional terrors is to live one day at a time.

- Self-honesty is essential to getting along with others in this world. Without stepping on others' toes, I need to check within to determine what I want in any given situation and express that. It just doesn't work for me to people-please, because I end up resenting the person or myself.

- Abstinence is the most important thing in my life without exception. It must be safeguarded and cherished. How can I do that? By working all of the steps every day and sharing my experience, strength, and hope with others.

I have grown and changed more in the last eleven years than in the previous twenty. Thanks to OA, the steps, and this wonderful Fellowship, I have a chance to have a fulfilling and meaningful life. Thanks to all of you for that gift.

Oakland, California

RECOVERY ROSTER

I know I'm in recovery because:

- I abstain from my trigger foods and have maintained my abstinence and weight loss for five and a half years.
- I stop eating when my body's had enough.
- I've quit weighing myself all the time.
- I go to social functions for the company of the people who'll be there and not for the huge amounts of food.
- Others can eat my binge foods in front of me, and I don't feel resentful; I can prepare my binge foods for others and not even be tempted to lick my fingers.
- I can live within my financial means, even when meager.
- Though disabled, I accept my health limitations without

crabbing about them continually.

- Instead of thinking about what I don't have, I'm truly grateful that I have so much.
- I don't make excuses to get out of going to meetings. Unless my health restricts me, I go whether I want to or not.
- I take the time to write, make phone calls, talk to my sponsor, and read OA literature, no matter how much I'd rather be doing something else.
- I can talk to my teenage son calmly when he's in the middle of a temper tantrum.
- When someone hurts me, I don't hold a grudge. I pray, let go, and let God.
- I recognize my character defects and am aware of how they hurt me and other people.
- I realize I can't always have my own way.
- I set healthy boundaries. I don't let people use me as a doormat, nor do I build walls that isolate me.
- I stay out of other people's business and let them run their own lives.
- Instead of "fixing" people I try simply to listen to them, sharing my experience, strength, and hope.
- I eliminate guilt and shame from my life, instead of merely saying, "That makes me feel guilty," and continuing to drag the guilt feelings around with me. I let the past go.
- I don't beat myself up when I make a choice that's not in my best interest; I learn from experience.
- I've stopped being a victim and started being a survivor.
- I accept being a grown-up and take responsibility for changing my actions and attitudes.
- I don't rely on anyone to make me happy, but realize that happiness comes from accepting God's will in my life.

Montague, Michigan

> I RECOGNIZE MY CHARACTER DEFECTS AND AM AWARE OF HOW THEY HURT ME AND OTHER PEOPLE.

PRESENT FOR LIFE

As I write this, I'm spending my vacation in sunny Florida with my family. This would be enviable, except for the reason I'm here. Three days ago, my mother and I received a call that my grandmother had taken very ill and might die at any time. So here I sit, looking at the ocean, while one of my closest relatives lies in the other room, dying.

I'm twenty-four years old. I've been abstinent almost two years, and I've seen my share of difficulties and accomplishments. I've been accepted at the university of my dreams, but all I can think about is graduation without granny.

This morning I sat on her bed, and we planned the colors for my wedding and what my dress should look like. Neither of us cared that I'm years away from that ceremony.

I'm grateful today for so many things, and I would like to share that gratitude with others — especially the newcomer who can't imagine being abstinent past today.

I'm incredibly grateful for not having my head in the fridge and my face in the toilet. Abstinence has allowed me to be here for my family and for granny. Before I left for Florida, my sponsor reminded me that a quick summary of the steps is "to grow up." For the first time, I feel very much a part of this family. They've included me in all the talks about granny's condition and have never treated me like a child.

I'm grateful I was able to say things to granny, and she was able to really hear and feel my love for her. If I were eating and throwing up, I'd be stuffing those feelings with tons of food. Five or ten years from now, I'd wish that I'd been able to tell her what she's meant to me. These feelings are very painful, but at last I can feel them. That means I'm really alive.

During the past couple of days, the compulsion has certainly been there. But my H.P. gives me the strength to deal with what may happen in the next twenty-four hours. I'm grateful for my concept of a loving H.P., who promises me that granny is going some place even more beautiful and peaceful than I could ever wish for her.

Thank you, *Lifeline*, OA, and H.P. for guiding me along a road of recovery to a place where I can support others as well as take care of my own needs.

San Diego, California

FINDING THE BALANCE

Before finding OA, I didn't know the meaning of the word "balance," and I didn't know that my life was unmanageable. I viewed the world in black-and-white extremes: Everything was either wonderful or awful, perfect or a total disaster. People were either good or bad, and I loved them or hated them. I was either wealthy or poverty-stricken, and of course, if I wasn't thin, I was fat.

And those misguided people in Overeaters Anonymous! Whenever I'd suggest one of my "perfect" solutions at a meeting, they'd debate and discuss it, and usually reject it. Like the time I suggested we use a non-Conference-approved book. When they turned down my sage advice, I was hurt, upset, and just plain mad!

Yet I kept going to meetings. There was nowhere else for me to go. I'd tried controlling my compulsive eating in many ways: diets, diet pills, rewards for losing weight (also known as compulsive spending), and starving. I'd lose weight, then put it back on plus more. I knew OA had answers for me because the people there said I had a disease. They said that I wasn't a bad person trying to become good, but a sick person trying to become well.

I KNEW OA HAD ANSWERS FOR ME BECAUSE THE PEOPLE THERE SAID I HAD A DISEASE.

Today I find that discussing differences of opinion helps me grow. At first when people in my OA group said, "Take what you like and leave the rest," I thought, "Yeah — I take it that you're crazy, and I'm leaving!" Now I'm learning to separate issues from personalities. Today it's okay for me to have opinions, values, and boundaries, and for others to have differing ones. It's also okay for me to change my ideas, and, later on, change them again.

Before OA I always thought I'd be happy "when." When I get thin. When I get married. When I get divorced. When I get a good job and make lots of money. When I retire. The "when" list went on and on.

Before OA I lived in grief, depression, disappointment, guilt, shame, and despair over past events. I decided I had to work the steps because I wanted the pain to go away.

Black-and-white thinking was one way I made my life unmanageable. Seeing the world in extremes kept me from people and from myself. Most of all, it kept me from having an intimate relationship with my Higher Power.

Today I can choose to go through problems rather than avoid them, seeing them as opportunities for growth. I recognize this world and the people in it as conduits through which my Higher Power contacts me.

Through OA I've found a way to be happy now. Call it whatever you want; acceptance, balance, growing up, "living life on life's terms." I call it being abstinent, in contact with my Higher Power, and living one day at a time.

Crystal Lake, Illinois

A ROSE WORTH THE THORNS

When I worked my first step, I was grateful to find "rose-colored abstinence." But as the weeks wore on, I found that the roses bore some thorns.

I kept telling my sponsor that I'd been slipping in my abstinence. Finally in the direct manner which I've come to love and respect, she said, "What's the difference, for you, between abstinence and dieting? Write about it!" I did, and I discovered some interesting things.

After I found my abstinence I swore I'd never diet again. But as time went on, abstinence became confusing. Abstinence, as I understand it, is to refrain from compulsive overeating. Dieting, on the other hand, is to control food intake, with the focus placed on calories and weight loss.

Abstinence is not only physical, but emotional and spiritual. If I'm abstinent, it's not by my control. But when I'm dieting, then I'm doing the controlling.

All my life thoughts about fattening foods have controlled my mind and emotions. So the question becomes: If I do eat some of those foods but remain abstinent, why do I feel guilty? Is it because true abstinence means I wouldn't even have a desire for those foods?

If I'm abstinent in all phases of my program, I don't desire those foods. Wanting to eat them is a sign that I'm not working my program — the compulsion is still there. They should be viewed as red flags. If I can rid myself of the guilt associated with eating those foods and focus on why I wanted them to begin with, the rest will fall into place. It sounds easy, but it's not.

> SOMETIMES IT SEEMS LIKE I'M ALWAYS WORKING AT IT, AND SOMETIMES I GET TIRED. THEN I ASK MYSELF, "ISN'T IT ALL WORTH IT — THE PROMISES, THE LIFTING OF MY COMPULSION?"

I don't ever want to diet again; yet I want it all, including physical recovery, and I want it now. Sometimes it seems like I'm always working at it, and sometimes I get tired. Then I ask myself, "Isn't it all worth it — the promises, the lifting of my compulsion?"

Abstinence can be confusing and hard, just like a lot of worthwhile things in life. But this goal is obtainable, and when I reach it, OA won't let me down as the diets did. All I have to do is be honest and willing. Sometimes that can be a tall order, but, after all, I'm worth it.

Edmonds, Washington

FEELING FULL

As an abstinent compulsive overeater, I always enjoy being comfortably hungry before each meal, and the feeling of satisfaction afterward. Occasionally I don't feel particularly hungry at mealtimes, but I eat anyway, because that's the best way I can maintain my three-meals-a-day abstinence.

But then there are rare times when I'm so full of feelings, generally negative ones, that I simply don't want to eat. Food tastes like cardboard and feels like a lead ball in my stomach — as if whatever I've eaten is too much and won't ever be digested.

I'm experiencing one of those times right now. I'm so focused on what might happen this coming weekend that I'm having trouble enjoying the richness of each moment and the miracle of abstinence at work in my body and my life.

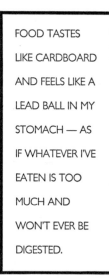

FOOD TASTES LIKE CARDBOARD AND FEELS LIKE A LEAD BALL IN MY STOMACH — AS IF WHATEVER I'VE EATEN IS TOO MUCH AND WON'T EVER BE DIGESTED.

I think the sensation of being "full of feelings" is a phenomenon unique to abstinence. I've been sixty pounds overweight and fifty pounds underweight at different times in my adult life. When I was anorexic, I was literally starving all the time. It wasn't that I ever had a moment when I didn't want to eat; I simply couldn't eat because I was so terrified of the food and the bingeing I knew I was capable of. Sure enough, self-starvation always led to uncontrollable bingeing, stuffing myself way beyond capacity and yet never feeling full. Or if I felt full, it certainly didn't affect my desire to eat more.

I'm grateful for the support of a wonderful sponsor and friends in the OA program who are there to listen to me and keep me grounded as I experience different levels of recovery. I'm grateful for my own willingness to listen to all my different hungers and the ability to differentiate between my body's needs and my disease, which tells me I'm too "full of feelings" to have room for healthy and abstinent meals.

I've spent the afternoon unraveling some of those feelings, working a few of the appropriate steps, and topping off my work with this article. As a result, I feel better about myself and have no intention of depriving myself of a delicious, well-balanced supper — or, better yet, a well-balanced life!

Washington, D.C.

INTENSIVE SELF-CARE

I 've discovered that having a certain amount of recovery doesn't mean that bad things won't happen to me anymore. What it does mean is that I don't have to make my troubles any worse by eating over them.

1991 was a very bad year for me. Three weeks into it, my mother was hospitalized. I flew back to New York with just enough clothes for a few days and a funeral. Instead, I wound up spending three weeks in a waiting room outside an intensive care unit.

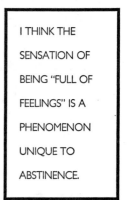

I THINK THE SENSATION OF BEING "FULL OF FEELINGS" IS A PHENOMENON UNIQUE TO ABSTINENCE.

During my hospital vigil, I wasn't able to prepare any meals for myself, yet I was able to eat abstinently the whole time. I ate in restaurants, relied on others to bring in food, and had lots of take-out meals. I don't ban any foods, but I do try to make most of my choices healthful. In this situation, that wasn't always possible.

Even though I wasn't able to get to a single OA meeting, the program sustained me during this ordeal. My Higher Power provided me with an OA buddy whose father was also in intensive care. I spent many nights burning up the phone lines to program friends in California. I wrote a lot and prayed even more. I read program literature and listened to tapes. Most importantly

I knew my Higher Power was there with me, and that's what got me through it.

When I returned to San Diego and stepped on the scale for the first time, I was amazed. Despite the weeks of inactivity and stress, my weight hadn't changed. It was a very valuable lesson. I'd been abstinent for four and a half years, but I'd never been tested like this.

Even if my food choices weren't those I would have made at home, I'd been able to feel, participate in life, and be there for my family. I hadn't succumbed to my disease, even back in the city where I'd first honed my compulsive eating skills.

> I DON'T BAN ANY FOODS, BUT I DO TRY TO MAKE MOST OF MY CHOICES HEALTHFUL.

My mother lived through this crisis, yet I knew it would only be a brief respite. Yesterday a message on my answering machine informed me that she had been admitted to a hospice. So I provoked an argument during dinner and didn't get to finish it. My compulsive thinking told me that I hadn't eaten enough, and that I should finish off with some dessert. There I was, staring at goodies in the freezer, when I realized with gratitude that no taste sensation would be able to take away my pain.

All I could do was share my feelings with my Higher Power, close the freezer door, and pick up the phone.

San Diego, California

PARTY PLAN

I was having a battle with myself, trying to decide whether or not to go to a kitchenware party. Parties like that tend to focus on the desserts served afterwards.

The guests gather around the overflowing table. A lot of attention is paid to who baked what and who's consuming it. And there's always a fuss made over those who choose not to eat. That lonely and isolated feeling is one I didn't want to experience.

After calling the hostess — a friend who is in another twelve-step program — I decided to go to the party. She told me that there wouldn't be great quantities of food on display, and I could leave to consume my planned abstinent meal.

At the party I let myself laugh and enjoy a game, not concentrating on the food items we shouted out as we played. It felt great to be with people I cared about, and I could feel their love for me as well.

But my happiness changed to anger as I revealed some of my current eating habits to a woman sitting next to me, a member of another twelve-step program. She was astonished to find that I choose not to eat certain foods and that I weigh and measure what I eat. (I knew most of the volume capacities of the containers being sold!) Her repeated exclamations of "You're so good. You never bake? You're so good!" stimulated my anger.

I told her that it has nothing to do with being "good" — it's what's necessary for me to stay abstinent. I knew she didn't understand. As I was putting on my coat she asked, "Doesn't it bother you to look at that dessert over there?" I replied, "Of course it bothers me, but it's my choice not to eat it and that's the best choice I can make."

I made a call when I got home. As I expressed my anger to a fellow compulsive eater, I began to cry. There's no way to get around the sense of loss I feel now that I'm abstinent. The sadness from missing the food and the emptiness from feeling different are there. But as long as I feel those feelings and don't pick up the food, I'll make it through another day.

I've worked hard to be blessed with a program that fills me with love. And if going through the pain is what it takes to stay in recovery and to help others, then so be it.

While taking my inventory that night, I recalled this woman had made oblique references to her own problems with overeating. It may be that exclaiming over my lifestyle was a way of denying her own experiences with food. Who knows? I fell asleep wondering if perhaps, without realizing it, I'd planted a seed.

Naugatuck, Connecticut

THE TEMPEST

A week ago our island of Kauai was devastated by a hurricane. I have to use the tool of writing today, since I am temporarily without regular meetings, my sponsor, and OA friends.

I waited twenty minutes at our OA meeting room (now converted to a Red Cross headquarters!), praying for someone to show up. As I drove away, I circled the block one last time and saw two OA friends walking towards the meeting room. We found a quiet place and had an OA meeting.

> A WEEK AGO OUR ISLAND OF KAUAI WAS DEVASTATED BY A HURRICANE. I HAVE TO USE THE TOOL OF WRITING TODAY, SINCE I AM TEMPORARILY WITHOUT REGULAR MEETINGS, MY SPONSOR, AND OA FRIENDS.

I was comforted to hear that they, too, were being urged to eat trigger foods and oversized, fatty meals by well-meaning friends and neighbors; they, too, had been tempted by offers of ice-cold beer and soda (we have to boil drinking water and very few people have any refrigeration); they, too, were committed to abstinence in a time of high stress and little choice of food and drink; they, too, struggled with honesty while filling out claim forms.

All the old justifications for compulsive overeating — eat now, there might not be food tomorrow; eat more, you need your strength; eat the rest, you can't afford to waste anything — were running amok in their minds, too. They, however, had made it to a meeting despite losing their homes and vehicles in the hurricane.

Life has changed drastically this week. But God still guides me. I have abstinence. I have the Fellowship of OA. I have everything I need to make it through the day.

Kauai, Hawaii

THE GHOST OF CHRISTMAS PAST

The holidays have always been a dismal time of year for me, mainly because my father died eight days before Christmas when I was nineteen. For most of my life my father and I weren't very close due to his alcoholism. During the last year of his life, however, he was recovering in AA both emotionally and spiritually, and I came to know him as the caring and loving person he could be.

When he died I felt that my Higher Power had taken away the father I had always wanted. Through the twelve steps of OA, I have come to realize that my H.P. had given me a wonderful gift — a short period of good times that left memories I can treasure the rest of my life.

Another aspect of Christmas past I've had to deal with is my attitude toward food. Before OA the only thing I looked forward to at Christmas was unrestricted eating. It was the one time of the year I could eat the way I wanted to and not feel guilty. In fact I felt that gorging myself on seasonal goodies was the expected behavior. I know better now, but it doesn't make abstinence easier.

DURING MY FIRST ABSTINENT CHRISTMAS I STRUGGLED TO KEEP AWAY FROM THE BINGE FOODS OF THE SEASON.

During my first abstinent Christmas I struggled to keep away from the binge foods of the season. I knew from my fourth step that I would be in for a rough time but followed my sponsor's advice to "go to meetings, pray, and not pick up that first compulsive bite." I stayed away from all social functions except for OA and AA, and even then I was cautious. I fought my toughest battles at work where there seemed to be an abundance of seasonal binge foods. To add to the torment, it appeared that everyone at work was attempting to force the junk on me against my wishes. I made it through that period abstinently, one day at a time, with the help of OA and my H.P. I now realize that it was nothing more than white-knuckle abstinence.

My second holiday season in OA was a much easier and more enjoyable experience. I used the same steps and tools that had kept me abstinent the rest of the year. The old binge foods were plentiful as ever but not an issue anymore. I sincerely didn't want any and felt good about it.

I was doubly grateful for the program when I noticed a colleague attempting to diet during the holiday season. Her struggle with food was the same as mine had been the previous year. What struck me most, however, was the look in her eyes. Although she was saying "No, thank you," with her mouth, her eyes were saying, "Please, give me some." I then fully comprehended the state of mind I had been in the previous Christmas. I now have an even greater appreciation for the gift I've been given by God and OA.

Coming up on my third Christmas in program, I'm full of excitement and hope. I'm taking a couple of beginner courses at the local community college, my work is more challenging and rewarding than I expected, I served as a delegate to Region 7 for my intergroup, and so far I've maintained my weight loss and my abstinence. None of this would be possible without H.P. and OA. I give credit to my sponsors who keep me honest and on an even keel.

I can't guarantee that I won't relapse tomorrow, next week, or next month, but I know what works for me and I'm grateful. This doesn't mean that my life always runs smoothly or that I'm a model of serenity, but it does mean that when I have to confront problems in my life, food is no longer an option.

Annapolis, Maryland

THE LAST WORD

In my first year of abstinence I lost weight quickly, then slowly put it back on again. In the last two years I have adjusted to the idea that I'm making permanent changes in my way of life, including — but not limited to — the changes in my eating behavior.

The hardest part of making these changes has been learning to live with the discomforts of an abstinent lifestyle. Giving up food, I've had to learn how to deal with pain, moods, and insecurities that only alter slowly.

There is, of course, joy in being abstinent. But the thrill of losing weight that marked early, pink-cloud abstinence passed away once I got into my goal-weight range. Then I found myself faced with the task of learning to live life on life's terms. That's when the tools came into play: sponsors, meetings, phone calls, and service.

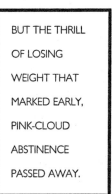

BUT THE THRILL OF LOSING WEIGHT THAT MARKED EARLY, PINK-CLOUD ABSTINENCE PASSED AWAY.

By using these tools during the last two years, I developed relationships with wonderful friends who taught me that abstinence works. They paid personal attention to me in my pain, insecurity, and moodiness. Their day-to-day victories over these same difficulties convinced me that staying abstinent is the best way to confront my own. When I yield to my illness, I multiply my problems instead of solving them.

In June I moved from Syracuse to Buffalo. Although this was my eighth move in twenty years, it is the first time that I've been abstinent and stayed abstinent throughout the process. Leaving my old friends behind hurts more than I ever thought it would. Feeling the pain of my loss and grieving for it is evidence of recovery. The pain itself reminds me how much I loved my friends and how much they meant to me. To numb the pain by overeating would cut me off from the knowledge of how much they meant to me, and I'm not willing to trade the intimacy I feel for food. Intimacy isn't instantaneous, however. I've had to work hard to make new friends in Buffalo, and there is still a lot to do to deepen these relationships.

There have been moments of joy in the transition. God lives in Buffalo, too, and there are lots of people here who know the joy of abstinence and share it at meetings. One Saturday in my new home group, a woman reminded me that abstinence is a tool, not a goal. The last woman to speak said that the pain we experience when we feel our feelings is much less than the pain we create by overeating. These messages helped me to stay abstinent at a time when I very much felt like taking my comfort in food.

> FEELING THE PAIN OF MY LOSS AND GRIEVING FOR IT IS EVIDENCE OF RECOVERY.

Although abstinence during the first few months after the move wasn't as easy as it's been at other times, I still treasure it. It sets me free to love my Higher Power, my friends, and myself I think of abstinence as the most powerful spiritual and mental action I can take to be joined to my friends in OA. We have real communion in recovery, even when we are separated by time and space.

Pain and joy may be mingled together in recovery, but joy has the last word.

Buffalo, New York

THE BASIS OF ABSTINENCE

I've been abstinent ten years, and I've seen many changes in OA and in myself. My pain and self-disgust were so profound when I joined that I was willing to do anything to feel better. I remember the emptiness — what seemed like endless time stretching between meals. In the beginning I was afraid of food, so I ate plainly and simply. I ate a lot of vegetables because I needed to feel full. I counted calories as a guide to quantity.

As my recovery became stronger my fear of food lessened. I ate a better variety, put cream in my coffee, and even tried some ex-binge foods. They didn't trigger a binge but were disappointing because the amount in a normal serving was so small. Some foods I never went back to, unwilling to risk my recovery for nothing but empty calories.

The twelve steps and my reliance on God are the basis upon which I maintain my abstinence. My understanding of God's will for me is whatever the sanest, healthiest choice at the time is. Never has that choice been compulsive overeating.

In the last few years more people have come from eating disorder units with very specific food plans. I see how hard they are on themselves if they deviate, and it reminds me of when I was so afraid of the food. I also notice a "which-comes-first" controversy — the emotions or the desire to overeat? I believe my repressed or unresolved negative emotions produce the desire to overeat and signal that something is wrong. I ask God to help me face whatever I'm trying to run away from. If I thought eating a "wrong" food caused my negative emotions, I'd just keep changing my food plan and never find out what really caused the feelings. I've learned a great deal about myself by putting my abstinence first, asking God for help in coping with reality, and trying to act on the insights I receive.

I also believe abstinence refers only to the food. I've been a basket case in OA; I've been filled with rage, severely depressed, irritable, hysterical, happy, miserable, and terrified. But I've never binged over those feelings. I've worked through them and gradually become somewhat less volatile. Letting emotions surface is part of the recovery process and it stems from abstinence. I can't numb myself anymore. I don't think abstinence means emotional stability — it doesn't give me serenity, it gives me reality.

Pittsburgh, Pennsylvania

AN OA LEXICON

How do I know when I've broken my abstinence? How do I tell the difference between relapse, slips, and simple weight gain?

My general rule for identifying slips is eating when I'm not hungry or eating inappropriate food when I am hungry.

I also distinguish between overeating, compulsive eating, and compulsive overeating.

Overeating is when I feel fine but the food tastes so good I eat more than I need. Or when I find it hard to say no to food that is offered to me. I realize that noncompulsive overeaters sometimes overeat too. Simple overeating can make me as fat as compulsive overeating, so it's important for me to think of ways I can protect myself against such situations or to counter overeating at one meal by eating less at my next one.

Compulsive eating is when I swallow my feelings with food. I don't eat more than I should and I don't eat anything that I consider unhealthy, but I don't process my feelings, I devour my food. I often think about one food while eating another.

> MENTALLY AND EMOTIONALLY I'M NOT OKAY, AND SO I TRY TO SOLVE MY PROBLEMS WITH FOOD.

Compulsive overeating is a problem of both what and why I'm eating. Mentally and emotionally I'm not okay, and so I try to solve my problems with food.

After many years of abstaining from compulsive overeating, I recently slipped. I was at a social event where I knew only the host and hostess, and feelings of alienation and inadequacy surfaced. Instead of reaching out to the other guests, I embraced the hors d'oeuvres. Not only was I overwhelmed with feelings, but my suffering was compounded by the feeling of heaviness the morning after. Although I had dulled my clarity, a corner of my sane self stayed with me and I was ashamed at having been out of control.

Writing about the experience made me realize the benefits of the abstinence I had taken for granted. But the price of this realization was too high. I don't want to revisit my pain in order to remember how awful it was. I would rather my slip hadn't happened, but it did happen and I dealt with it by telling my group about it when I took my fourteen-year candle.

If I'm in relapse I don't talk about it. I compound the problem by beating myself up. I refuse to take remedial action. I refuse to learn from it, and I continue to sabotage myself by not reaching out. I've given up. I cooperate with my craziness. Relapse starts long before I take that first compulsive bite. It begins with the stinking thinking of cockiness or low self-esteem. It ends with increasing isolation and weight gain.

Simple weight gain is due to physical causes such as medication or eating something with more calories than I can assimilate. Sometimes it happens when my food intake remains the same but I curtail my exercise because of sickness or scheduling. Whatever the cause, I deal with it.

Hawthorne, California

AMONG FRIENDS

I'm an independent woman. For thirty years before joining OA, I was convinced that if I had an idea and made up my mind to work toward that end, I could achieve anything. College, marriage, a career in education, worldwide travel, and even a marathon were among the personal goals I had reached. Yet I could not overcome the obsession with food, the progression of weekly then daily binges, the weight that kept climbing.

Diets, acupuncture, water pills, fasting, ad infinitum! Short periods of successful dieting were always followed by long periods of demoralizing behavior with food. I wanted a way out, but on my own I couldn't see a solution.

The AA Twelve and Twelve tells us that many who tried AA "did not succeed because they could not make the admission of hopelessness." Fortunately, by the time I got to Overeaters Anonymous, I was without hope, and had no sane thoughts or behaviors where food was concerned. I may not have known what would work to free me from the obsession, but I was very clear on what didn't.

Father Ed Dowling, a dear friend of AA in its early years, once said that if he were to get to heaven it would be through no virtue of his own. He would find himself there simply as a result of backing out of hell. This describes my introduction to OA and abstinence perfectly. I was simply backing away from the hell of compulsive overeating. And as I abstained, worked the steps, and used the tools, I woke up one day to find myself in recovery.

My abstinence was defined by what didn't work. Second helpings were out. If I knew that going back for more was an option, then half way through the first helping, I would be thinking about the second one. After that "more" was never enough.

MY ABSTINENCE WAS DEFINED BY WHAT DIDN'T WORK.

The foods that called to me were very clear in my mind. I knew which foods I needed to avoid within my three meals. And honesty continues to keep me from thinking that I can "handle" these foods after a certain period of abstinence.

The hopelessness I felt nearly seven years ago gave birth to new life: a life of recovery that goes beyond my wildest dreams. I'm still an independent woman, though now I have enough sense to know that I wasn't intended to journey alone. Each day I must walk with my Higher Power and each of you, my lifelines of support in the journey without compulsive overeating.

Corona del Mar, California

ISLAND OASIS

I went to my first OA meeting three and a half years ago with two dreams. The first was to stop compulsively overeating, the second was to travel. So far in recovery, I've kept off thirteen pounds and been around the world.

After eighteen months in the program, I had lost ten pounds and had just landed a new job teaching college-level English to members of the navy — while deployed on a tender taking care of combat ships in the Persian Gulf! As I prepared to leave the

States, I had no idea what to expect nor even what countries my ship would be visiting as that information was classified. The only instructions I got were that I couldn't wear skirts on board!

Naturally, I was sad to leave my wonderful home OA group, my sponsors, and the members I was sponsoring, but I planned to take my program with me. I'd heard that many ships had twelve-step meetings (usually AA) nightly, but I suspected that my classes would probably meet in the evenings, too, when the sailors were off duty. I worried about whether I'd be able to make the meetings, and whether I could work an OA program with only AAs for support. In typical fashion, I found myself worrying needlessly about the following month's schedule of a ship on the other side of the world!

The flight to the Philippines took nineteen hours. After a brief rest, I got onto a military plane full of sailors and we headed for our next stop, Diego Garcia. Diego Garcia is a tiny island seven degrees south of the equator in the middle of the Indian Ocean. As we landed, the island looked like a scene from *South Pacific*: a coconut grove bordering a clean white beach curving around a horseshoe-shaped bay. We were dying to get in the water, but everyone from the plane had to wait in a huge processing room. There were sailors from dozens of ships, and everyone's paperwork had to be processed in the maddeningly slow way of the military.

SHE SMILED AND TAPPED HER DAILY MEDITATION BOOK. "MY HIGHER POWER IS REALLY HELPING ME OUT," SHE SAID.

In the midst of hundreds of blue and white uniforms, I happened to take a seat behind a woman just as she opened her briefcase to reveal OA pamphlets! I leaned forward and whispered, "I think we have something in common — I'm a compulsive overeater." She smiled and tapped her daily meditation book. "My Higher Power is really helping me out," she said. "I was praying to meet someone here." Amazingly, it turned out that we were en route to the same ship.

We planned to attend an AA meeting together that night on Diego Garcia. I needed one. The temperature was over 100 degrees and the bay that had looked so inviting turned out to be only two feet deep and as warm as the air. After a day of walking in the jungle, fighting off the fat, ferocious mosquitoes and paddling in two feet of hot water, I refused a few invitations to the officers' club and took my sunburned body to the AA meeting.

There were three other people there as delighted to see us as we were to see them as they don't get many visitors. The island is notoriously boring for people stationed there and heavy drinking is the main activity. The three men we met that night were struggling to recover in the midst of that insanity — and doing a good job.

> SHARING THE STRUGGLE OF STAYING SERENE IN SUCH HARSH CONDITIONS, WE HELPED EACH OTHER THROUGH HOMESICKNESS AND HOME-MEETING SICKNESS.

Once I reached my ship I learned that the AA meetings were held at 8 PM, right in the middle of my classes. But my shipmate and I started an OA group that met whenever we felt the need — often every day!

Navy ships, I soon discovered, are noisy and crowded places with a lot of unhappy people packed much too close together. This crew had been out to sea for four months, not even catching a glimpse of land for more than sixty days. Low morale showed everywhere. Meals in the officers' wardroom were depressing and silent (I was never tempted to prolong them), and my students, though eager to learn, were exhausted by the endless work of supporting the smaller ships.

Worst of all, we were at anchor, and the ship's weak air conditioning was no competition for the sun baking our metal ship. Some of my students worked in the engine room in 140-degree heat. The temperature on deck, where a few of us sweated through aerobics, was usually 110 to 120 degrees. Down below in the crew's berthing, the heat was barely tolerable. After teaching, I would go on deck in search of a little coolness, but the night air was as hot as the day's.

Because no alcohol was allowed on board, sugar was the drug of choice. In every office or shop I'd see sailors munching sweet junk food. The supply chief told me that one of his biggest problems was keeping the ship stocked with sodas since the 1,100-person crew each drank an average of five cans a day!

Since I couldn't have visitors in my stateroom, my OA friend and I met in her office. This tiny metal cubbyhole with harsh lights, no ventilation, and only a thin divider separating us from two other rooms, became our sanctuary. Sharing the struggle of staying serene in such harsh conditions, we helped each other through homesickness and home-meeting sickness. Before taking this job I'd aided my abstinence by giving myself treats other than food: baths, walks, flowers, and occasionally new clothes or cosmetics.

The problem was none of these things were available on board. We only had the Big Book, OA literature, our Higher Power, and each other — and it worked! My abstinence was as clean then as it's ever been.

My time on the tender ended suddenly. One hot night I moved to the upper bunk in hopes of getting some cool air from the fan. At 3 AM my phone rang and I, half asleep and forgetting that I'd changed beds, jumped to get it. I fell seven feet onto one-and-a-half-inch plate steel, breaking my right wrist. People heard my screams several decks away.

Twenty-four hours later, with one arm in a cast and my bags packed, I stood on deck wearing a lifejacket, a hard hat, and a harness, waiting to be hoisted off the ship by means of a crane inside one of the huge metal boxes usually used for burning garbage. My OA and AA friends showed up, having slipped away from their duties to say goodbye. We held hands and said the Serenity Prayer. I stepped into the burn box and began my long, painful journey home. The program goodbye was a good start, and I knew that thanks to OA and the worldwide twelve-step Fellowship, I would never be alone.

San Diego, California

PROMISING STEPS

Shortly after coming to OA almost three years ago I began to notice a change in my attitudes toward social gatherings, particularly parties. I found myself feeling increasingly uncomfortable at these events, and frequently wished I had stayed home. Dinner parties, birthday parties, holiday parties . . . I began to avoid them whenever possible. Unfortunately this became a problem at home since my wife loves parties and we are frequently invited to them.

Instead of examining my feelings, I justified my stance by rationalizing that refusing to attend parties was "taking care of myself." After all, I thought, parties are just food and alcohol feasts that have no place in my daily eating plan. I was partially correct. When I first gained my abstinence, parties were slippery places for me because of the unlimited food and drink. But as time went on and my recovery progressed, I realized that what made me uncomfortable at parties was my uneasiness with myself and the other guests — not the food.

In the days before I came to OA, I ate and drank my way through parties, thus avoiding having to confront my feelings. Anger, low self-esteem, and fear of people were the underlying causes of my overeating at parties. I often felt less than others, believing I had nothing interesting or important to say. I was also uncomfortable about my 315-pound body, so I preferred not to talk to anyone, convinced they would judge me by my size. These feelings also precipitated my anger, and I actually found myself resenting people who could enjoy themselves.

When I reached a normal weight and remained abstinent, these feelings that had been buried. began to resurface. No wonder I didn't like parties — they brought to light some of my most serious defects of character. It was clear that there was work to be done, and the program provided the answer.

I asked H.P. for help with this problem, and resolved to go to the next party with an open mind, willing to confront my discomfort. The first party I attended was tough as my wife was unable to go and I'd always depended on her to keep me company. When I walked in the door I realized that I didn't know anyone in the room — and all eyes were on me. I was fearful, but I remembered to trust my plan. After the host introduced me to others around the room, I told a few jokes and began to feel more at ease than usual. I saw the spread of food and alcohol but thought, "It's not for me" and chose a diet drink instead. I began getting to know the other guests, moving from person to person. Eventually some people I knew arrived and I felt even more comfortable, but I realized that it really didn't matter, as my Higher Power and I were doing just fine on our own.

One of the promises of the steps was at work: I found myself intuitively knowing how to handle a situation that used to baffle me. I felt comfortable instead of afraid. Later on we played a party game (which I'd always hated) and I won! I really had a good time. For the other guests it was probably just another party, but for me, it was a breakthrough.

I continue to share my feelings about parties at meetings and with my sponsor because they are a symbol of many other problems I have in my life. My uncomfortable feelings haven't totally disappeared, but they are definitely getting less intense. I don't go to every party that comes along, but I go to many more than before — and I enjoy most of them. My wife has certainly noticed the difference too.

Looking to the program for a solution was the key to my growth in this regard, and it served to strengthen my abstinence — and my belief in the OA twelve-step way of life.

Washington, D.C.

STEADY AS SHE GOES

For a woman who's not particularly fond of changes, I feel I've had my full share these past twelve months. Changes come in many forms, and whether positive or negative, they rock my emotional boat. Many days I've had to remind myself that no matter what happens, as long as I don't take that first compulsive bite, everything will be okay.

Just a year ago I was living with my family, helping them with their business, dating several nice men, enjoying the friendship of my girlfriends, and, as always, staying close to twelve-step programs. But all of a sudden, everything around me was in a state of flux — even my dreams were unsettling.

Then several months ago my father died of cancer. When my sister told me, she and I talked, cried, and attempted to comfort each other. Our family has never been a particularly close one, but my sister and I have gone to great lengths to build and preserve a loving relationship. We grew up with alcoholism and all the ramifications of that disease.

I miss my dad very much. Ours was a special bond in that he got sober in AA nearly seven years ago. Sobriety is the greatest gift that my father gave me. And I began to recover during those years too. That was a gift I gave my dad.

SOBRIETY IS THE GREATEST GIFT THAT MY FATHER GAVE ME. AND I BEGAN TO RECOVER DURING THOSE YEARS TOO. THAT WAS A GIFT I GAVE MY DAD.

The last time I saw him, we'd each checked our own side of the street, made any necessary amends, thanked each other for recovery, and said good-bye with an "I love you."

Unfortunately, most of the rest of my family has asked me not to come around any more. They don't understand twelve-step programs. And with my dad gone, perhaps they'd rather pretend the programs don't exist.

It's been painful. When the feelings of sadness and grief are strong, I call upon my God for strength, power, and sanity, and I am comforted and protected. I look to the tools for help in walking through the feelings without excess food. Prayer, reading, phone calls, writing, and three abstinent meals provide the needed structure to my day.

There have been positive aspects this past year. I met a man in AA. We became engaged and now are living together very happily. I also began writing full time, and am grateful to report that my work is being published regularly. As a plus, my fiance is a photojournalist, so we make a great team professionally, too. it's been a challenging year, full of many changes. But what has remained constant is my abstinence. I found that keeping to the basics of the program — and avoiding that first bite — led to a sense of stability when I desperately needed it.

The program is my calm in the storm. And when the winds subside, I'm still a complete person. And, by the grace of God, still in recovery.

Corona del Mar, California

SAFE AND SANE

I have just completed a two-week vacation without going crazy or breaking my abstinence. Surely a miracle!

I spent the first week studying at a music and art school. Pre-OA, I never even attempted such a thing: I just "knew" that everyone else would be more experienced and competent than I, not to mention thinner.

Well, I'm not thin yet, but I'm no longer afraid. And I was fit enough to manage getting around on a campus where everything seemed to be on a hill!

I did the footwork regarding my abstinence, calling the school before I left so I would have a fairly accurate idea of what kinds of food would be available. During the week, before each meal, I read the menu printed on the board outside the cafeteria, said a prayer for help, and then made sane choices.

That week I was invited to a potluck dinner. Such open, unrestricted displays of food make me uncomfortable. Inwardly, I would hear my disease screaming at me to sample everything. To take care of myself, I ate my abstinent dinner beforehand and wandered over to the get-together later. Without the distraction of food (I stayed away from the loaded tables), I enjoyed the fellowship of the students. The following morning, two potluck goers complained of being overstuffed; how grateful I was that I didn't share their problem.

I spent the second week of my vacation in a strange city at the home of a friend I hadn't seen for six years. Initially I was reluctant to open up to her about my abstinence needs since I didn't want to be a nuisance. But once I explained my food plan to her, she was happy to accommodate me.

> I SPENT THE FIRST WEEK STUDYING AT A MUSIC AND ART SCHOOL. PRE-OA, I NEVER EVEN ATTEMPTED SUCH A THING.

During my stay I wanted to attend some OA meetings. Despite my anxiety about driving in uncharted territory, I prayed for strength and I found it. Although the Big Book reference to "going to any length" doesn't literally mean in miles, I faced a welter of freeways to get to OA meetings. I let my willingness guide me. And whenever I lost my way, I simply pulled off the rood, checked my map, and went on. It's exactly the way I work my program — no wonder it works!

My experiences prove that a good vacation is nothing more than an extension of a sane and serene life.

NEW WAY OF LIVING

My husband travels on business about three or four times a year. I used to do some of my worst bingeing while he was out of town. The loneliness and boredom were more than I could bear, and I ate in an effort to fill the emptiness. I felt I deserved to eat in order to comfort myself.

How things have changed! After four years of working an OA program, I now handle my husband's business trips quite differently. The most important change is that I stay abstinent. I don't use his absence as an excuse to binge. When he's gone, I attend extra meetings to remind myself of my disease, and to be with people who can hug me and help me feel less lonely. I nurture myself spiritually by working the steps, by praying, and by attending my church. And I engage in fun, meaningful, and fulfilling activities.

During my husband's most recent absence, I happened upon an idea that may become a regular tradition. I invited three OA friends to my home for a potluck. After an abstinent dinner, we sat in my living room for three hours, talking, sharing, and laughing. It was like having a meeting in my own home.

It's just another example of the many healthy ways I've learned to take care of myself.

Chapel Hill, North Carolina

LIVIN' IT UP!

I just returned from a vacation in Orlando, Florida. I acted like any normal, healthy thirteen-year-old, running from one Epcot Center exhibit to another, petting animals at the Busch Gardens petting zoo, and going on rides at Walt Disney World. H.P. really gave me a chance to enjoy a vacation like a teenager was meant to.

The catch? I'm a thirty-three-year-old recovering compulsive overeater.

As a teenager, I was depressed and unhappy and I didn't know why. I felt so different from everyone else, and I was sure that no one would like me if they knew the real me (whoever that was). I thought my feelings of ugliness, unacceptability, and separateness were mine alone.

How different my life is because of OA. Now I can share my most intimate thoughts and feelings with another person and know that I am understood, loved, and supported. After eleven years of recovery, seven years of abstinence, and having maintained a seventy-five-pound weight loss, Higher Power is helping me to do things that I never thought I could do for myself. Namely, being able to vacation in Florida for a week and stay abstinent and sane.

> WORKING MY PROGRAM HAS ALSO GIVEN ME THE POWER OF CHOICE WITH REGARD TO FOOD.

I enjoyed the fun, the sun, the entertainment, and the people. I wore shorts and halter tops during the morning and lounged around the pool in a bathing suit all afternoon. Rather than focusing on my problems and my self-centered negativity, I chose instead to focus on the positiveness of the people, places, and things I encountered.

Working my program has also given me the power of choice with regard to food. I used to feel I had to eat my binge foods. I used to believe that food talked to me. I used to think I couldn't say no. Not anymore. Thanks to OA, food is no longer my Higher Power.

Boise, Idaho

YOU CAN TAKE IT WITH YOU

I am aware of the many gifts of this program as I enjoy my second abstinent summer. I have been relieved of the dread that used to precede the change of seasons and the inevitable wardrobe change that went with it — from comfortably bulky wool to cool, revealing cotton. The dread has been lifted because of the self-acceptance I have been blessed with through the program.

I have also been relieved of the insanity that used to possess me as I prepared for vacations. No more compulsive dieting, obsessive exercising, or frantic shopping for something to wear. Now, I pack only the clothes that fit, abandoning the idea that I could certainly knock off a few pounds while I'm away.

I'm especially careful about packing my program, because without it, my vacation would be a living hell. I make sure to take my literature, my journal, the most recent issue of *Lifeline*, and phone lists.

Probably the most important item I bring is willingness. I must be willing to get down on my knees and turn my will and my life over to my Higher Power first thing every morning, even while on vacation. I must be willing to spend time reading my literature, and to take advantage of leisure time to listen to what H.P. has to say. I must be willing to look up Overeaters Anonymous in the phone book and make contact with another compulsive overeater.

I recently returned from Virginia Beach after visiting my brother and his wife. I was glad to be with them during the birth of their daughter. While there, I enjoyed walks along the shore and bike rides around the lake. I felt quite comfortable wearing shorts, something I didn't feel worthy of before program.

Actually, my first vacation miracle happened about one year ago, when H.P. made it possible for me to go to Italy for six weeks, combining my medical training with a vacation. And the gift of abstinence was given to me each day as I turned everything over to God — going to meetings, making new program friends in Milan, and even writing a portion of my fourth-step inventory and taking the fifth step with a woman who will always be so special to me.

> PROBABLY THE MOST IMPORTANT ITEM I BRING IS WILLINGNESS. I MUST BE WILLING TO GET DOWN ON MY KNEES AND TURN MY WILL AND MY LIFE OVER TO MY HIGHER POWER FIRST THING EVERY MORNING, EVEN WHILE ON VACATION.

God willing, I hope to return to Italy at the end of this summer. I know that my disease will travel with me, so, gratefully, I'll choose to take my program along too.

Philadelphia, Pennsylvania

ABSTINENCE HAS NO BOUNDARIES

Five years ago, when I was first deciding what my abstinence would be, I followed my own personal guidelines. First, my abstinence had to be livable. To me, that meant I could continue it for a lifetime. Secondly, I had to be able to eat out and still maintain my abstinence. Thirdly, I had to be able to eat abstinently anywhere in the world.

Two years later, and newly at maintenance weight, that third part came in very handy when I learned my husband had received orders to go to Japan for three years. I was so excited about the move. I worried about many things, but oddly enough, abstinence wasn't one of them. I trusted God to be wherever I was.

Our first six weeks in Japan were spent in a hotel until we could find a house. Unable to cook, I ate out three meals a day. With abstinence as my first priority, it was an adventure. At the very least, it was an immediate incentive to learn a little Japanese so I could order or buy the food I needed.

When we moved into our new house, I began making the two-hour trip into Tokyo for OA meetings. By telephone, I began to build the support system that was to sustain me for the next three years. I got two OA pen pals through OA's pen pal program. Writing to those OAs became my between-meeting opportunities to strengthen my program.

When traveling, most people have a tendency to want to taste new and exotic foods. I knew that wasn't for me, so I decided I'd find my joy in the people, the country, and the culture. I didn't want my experience spoiled by a return to my illness.

Japanese women, as I was to discover, love to extend hospitality with food, so I was often in the position of having to refuse food. At first, I learned how to say, "I don't eat sugar," in Japanese, but then they were confused when I refused nonsugar foods. I learned to explain my three-meal-a-day abstinence. Sometimes I showed my fat pictures, and explained that I didn't want to return to my former size. Eventually, my friends learned to offer me only coffee or tea.

The most humorous experience in this regard was when one Japanese friend asked me why, after three years of "dieting" (her understanding of my abstinence), did I still look the same? I hadn't considered that it would confuse anyone if I said I was on a diet. She'd probably wondered why I just didn't give up — or at least try a more successful "diet"!

I'm so thankful for my early years in OA when I had heard other members say, "My disease doesn't take a vacation from me, so I can't take a vacation from abstinence." Since I didn't want to lose my abstinence during my time in Japan, I used the tools, worked the steps, and left the rest to God. Fortunately, I was never afraid to ask my hostesses for help in meeting my abstinence needs. I didn't have to be ashamed of my disease.

I came home a few months ago. I hadn't changed in size, but inside I had grown. I am so grateful I have a portable program, and I can carry it anywhere.

Olympia, Washington

VACATION WITH A DIFFERENCE

ifeline's request for articles on vacation experiences touched several chords in me. So here's my story.

Pre-OA, I had gone to my mother-in-law's on vacation many times. During those trips, I had felt bored, sluggish, restless, irritable, and uninterested in anything except going to restaurants. I had also made several "diet" trips to her home, when I was consumed with not eating, getting thinner, and checking my weight.

I vividly remember how bowled over I was by the differences between those trips and my first abstinent vacation there. I enjoyed this last trip so much. I felt centered and peaceful, displayed much more tolerance toward my mother-in-law, enjoyed brisk walks, and felt brave enough to go to unfamiliar OA meetings.

Even though I'm now thin, I still don't feel good in a bathing suit because I have a pot belly that just plain shows in clingy lycra! But I've come to accept that it's not important enough to me to try to exercise it away, so when I go to the beach, I just wear skimpy shorts and a shirt, or something else that I feel good wearing. I've grown in acceptance of my body in OA. Thanking my body for serving me so well has helped.

> SINCE VACATION SCHEDULES CAN BE JAM-PACKED AND CONFUSING, I TRY TO DO MY DAILY PRAYER AND MEDITATION BEFORE STIRRING OUT OF BED IN THE MORNING. I NEVER TAKE A VACATION FROM GOD.

When visiting relatives on vacation, I've sometimes had to stand up for my right to refrain from sugar. I've found it helps to tell them that the foods they've prepared look terrific, but that I can't eat them — not even a small bite — because I want to treat myself well. It helps to explain that sugar is as seductive to me as booze may be for an alcoholic. Often, people will comment on how "good" I am to refuse dessert. In this case, I say that it's not a moral issue for me, but rather a matter of sanity and survival. I feel comfortable being open about this. At times it leads to interesting conversations and twelfth-step work.

Since vacation schedules can be jam-packed and confusing, I try do my daily prayer and meditation before stirring out of bed in the morning. I never take a vacation from God.

It also helps me to remember to accept my feelings while on vacation; just because I'm away from home doesn't mean I'm always happy and having fun. In fact, heightened expectations can lead to just the opposite: confusion, depression, and loneliness. Also, I try to stay open and vulnerable to the people I'm with, and look to them, rather than food, for the emotional comfort, closeness, and friendship I desire. I've found there's always some of God visible in the love of others.

Bryn Athyn, Pennsylvania

FLYING HIGH WITH OA

I'm on my way to London, literally, so it seems like a good time to share a bit about how I stay abstinent on the road — and in the air.

Airline seats have become a lot more comfortable since I lost 100 pounds (compliments of OA). However, I need to work my OA program just as intensely now as I did when I was first losing that weight six years ago.

Lots of OA meetings are just as essential to me while traveling as when I'm at home because my eating disorder travels with me. In fact, I have a London OA meeting list with me, thanks to one of my sponsorees who was there last month.

Food selection while traveling can present some difficulties. Travel schedules, work responsibilities, time differences, and local food availability can make it hard to obtain my preferred foods. Nevertheless, I don't deviate from the basic structure of my food plan. Through many years of trial and error, I have discovered an eating plan that works best for me, and I stick to it. For me, it is much easier to stay abstinent than to get abstinent.

Airlines are quite willing to provide me with a special meal if given advance notice. However, they make mistakes regularly, as they did today. So as a back-up, I carry some abstinent foods on board to eat on such occasions.

Prayer, meditation, reading the Big Book, attending OA meetings, and sending postcards to OA friends back home are just some of the actions I take to stay abstinent on the road. Even transatlantic phone calls are cheaper than bingeing. And if I'm lucky, I'll find someone with whom I can share my program, because working with other compulsive overeaters is the best guarantee I have.

Oakland, California

Seven

HOW ABSTINENCE CHANGES WITH
TIME AND EXPERIENCE

BLESSED EVENT

Having been blessed with abstinence and physical recovery, being pregnant made me view my program in an entirely new way.

Out went my three-meals-a-day abstinence. Being blighted with nausea for three months made me ask God for the willingness to be more flexible with my food. My abstinence changed each day as my pregnancy progressed. It felt comfortable because my food was being controlled by God.

Back came the scale into my life. My own had been thrown out long ago. Now doctors and midwives needed to monitor my weight gain. At first this terrified me, bringing back feelings and memories associated with diet clubs. But I shared my fears honestly with my sponsoree, and, after the first weigh-in, the fears dissolved.

> IT FELT COM-
> FORTABLE
> BECAUSE MY
> FOOD WAS
> BEING CON-
> TROLLED BY
> GOD.

Once more I had to deal with an expanding waistline. I had trouble separating feelings of what a swelling stomach meant in the past from what it means in pregnancy. All those old emotions of guilt and remorse after a binge needed to be dealt with promptly.

The discomfort of tight waistbands meant the baby was getting bigger, not me! But switching to elasticized pants and baggy tops and putting "normal" clothes away for the future made me think of my pre-OA days. I had to remind myself that I live each day in recovery lovingly supported by OA friends. This expansion in my body meant a new life — for me as well as the baby.

I gave birth to a beautiful baby daughter. In God's timing, the gift of physical recovery returned as though it had never disappeared. Maybe to God it had been there all along.

Nottingham, England

OPENING WINDOWS

Last summer we started renovating our big, old house. I'd been in OA for three years, had lost eighty pounds, and was enjoying a clean abstinence, one day at a time.

I was excited about getting a new kitchen and bathroom. The old ones were dark and cramped, and I longed to knock down the old walls, put in lots of beautiful new windows, and bring in some sunshine and fresh air.

During the construction I struggled with my eating. It was hard to stay abstinent, I rationalized, because my kitchen was all torn up, and I couldn't cook properly. The stress of the expense of the project and the unexpected delays and complications made it hard for me to meditate and exercise.

DURING THE CONSTRUCTION I STRUGGLED WITH MY EATING.

When it was completed the house was beautiful, and I was twenty pounds heavier and desperate to find a way back to the serenity I had once enjoyed.

As I struggled, my Higher Power reminded me of the windows I had needed in my home. I realized that I need to open windows, one day at a time, to work my OA program as well.

When I call my sponsor, it feels as if I've opened a window and let in the fresh morning air. When I take time to read OA literature and meditate, the warm sunshine of understanding shines on my face.

Whenever I go to a meeting, I feel like I'm opening a window that lets me see where I'm going and where I've been.

I used to feel that "working my program" was indeed work. But now it's as easy to me as opening windows — and how much joy, strength, and comfort I get from living with sunshine and fresh air! I realize that I want to use the tools of the program — my beautiful windows — every day.

Minneapolis, Minnesota

PERFECTION NOT REQUIRED

One night I walked away from the dinner table discouraged, my body sluggish from too much food, and my heart lonely. I'd been abstinent for three and a half years, lost more than 100 pounds, and hadn't felt this way since before I joined OA.

I wasn't eating my binge foods or eating between meals. But the meals were becoming too big. Why? I realized that nearly six weeks had passed since I'd attended a meeting. And I remembered many phone calls from concerned OA friends that I'd failed to return. I was still reading my literature and writing in my journal every day, but apparently this wasn't enough.

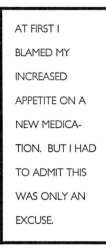

AT FIRST I BLAMED MY INCREASED APPETITE ON A NEW MEDICA-TION. BUT I HAD TO ADMIT THIS WAS ONLY AN EXCUSE.

At first I blamed my increased appetite on a new medication. But I had to admit this was only an excuse. I'd been using a recurring illness to isolate myself, and that was leading me back to my old friend and enemy, food.

Dealing with the illness was difficult enough; now I was slipping back into old habits. Did I have the strength to change? Writing in my journal helped me realize that I didn't need strength — what I needed was the willingness to admit my powerlessness, ask for help, and begin anew.

I asked my Higher Power to help me. I committed to attending at least one meeting a week. I began making phone calls. I wrote down my food every day (something I never had to do before) and continued to read and write. Every morning, I turned my will over to my Higher Power, and every evening I went to bed grateful for another good program day.

As I write this, a month has passed. It's now spring. The air is crisp and clear, the leaves are budding anew, and so is my life. My health is only slightly better, but once again I feel connected. I'm going to meetings, using the phone, and staying abstinent. And, best of all, I'm grateful to have a program that allows me to recover even when I'm less than perfect.

Quincy, Massachusetts

RELAPSE HAPPENS

I used to hear, "Relapse is a part of recovery," and discount it because I thought it meant that everyone is going to relapse sooner or later. I learned that it's a paraphrase for "Relapse happens."

Why do people relapse? Is relapse avoidable? Is it inevitable? These questions are all so meaningless because the only thing that matters is that relapse does happen. Debate over the legitimacy of relapse only serves to shame us and — as we all know — shame never motivated any of us to do anything but hide and eat. We need acceptance instead of debate.

I thought relapse would never happen to me. I was working the steps, measuring my food, calling my sponsor — what could go wrong? When I hit goal weight I started to slip. I hung on to my old ideas about abstinence, program, and relapse until I choked the very life out of them, only letting on at meetings that I was having "a little trouble with my food." I wondered where my Higher Power was. It was when I finally accepted that I was in relapse that I felt my H.P.'s presence again. I felt a hand on my shoulder and the beginning of the most spiritual journey in my recovery. I learned that God's love is absolutely unconditional. No matter what I've done, where I'm at, or what I'm putting in my mouth, my H.P. is right there letting me know that I'm accepted and I must accept myself (and others) in the same way. My Higher Power is always in the present moment. Since I couldn't accept that I was in relapse, I wasn't living in the present and couldn't find my

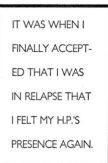

IT WAS WHEN I FINALLY ACCEPTED THAT I WAS IN RELAPSE THAT I FELT MY H.P.'S PRESENCE AGAIN.

Higher Power. I got back in touch with the reality of the moment, and I learned to value my abstinence for the miracle that it really is.

Could I have avoided relapse? I don't know. But I don't regret it. It taught me that weighing and measuring is not the only way to be abstinent, that it's not true that only abstinent people have something of value to say, and that arrogance is an immediate food-trigger for me. The experience solidified my trust in H.P.'s presence in good times and bad, made me a humbler, gentler person, and got me back in touch with the meaning of "fellow sufferers." It also made me a more seasoned sponsor. The way to sponsor people in relapse is to give them exactly what my H.P. gave me, to let them know that I accept them unconditionally — without judgment — and encourage them to keep coming back.

Schenectady, New York

WHEN YOU WORK IT

"Hi, my name is Elizabeth, and I'm a compulsive overeater." In my three years in OA I've said that over 1,000 times. I know what it means, too: It means I'm powerless over food; I have an eating disorder. It also means that I'm a member of Overeaters Anonymous, the program that saved my life.

When I came to OA I probably weighed over 325 pounds, although my top recorded weight was 312. Most, if not all, of the weight I'd lost on a recent diet was back on my five-foot frame. At that height and weight, I was someone little kids pointed at — when I went out, which was as little as possible.

In spite of this, it wasn't really the desire to lose weight that brought me to and kept me in OA. At the point when I found the program, I was hurting so badly that I was willing to try anything.

I'd quit my teaching job to open a business with a friend, and it had failed. I had enough retirement money to live on for a year, and was actively planning to commit suicide when the money ran out. After all — who would hire someone who weighed over 300 pounds and was a failure? Besides, I'd been told all my life that I'd be dead from obesity by the time I was forty, and I was thirty-eight at the time.

I'd gone to an OA meeting seven or eight years before, but the people there kept talking about Jesus, and as a Jewish atheist I wanted nothing to do with what seemed to be a program for Christians. At that time I didn't know that this is not a religious program, but a spiritual one, and that my Higher Power could be whatever I chose it to be. I also wasn't hurting badly enough then to be willing to go to any lengths.

> I ALSO WASN'T HURTING BADLY ENOUGH THEN TO BE WILLING TO GO TO ANY LENGTHS.

I'd been in therapy a few weeks when it was suggested that I try a different twelve-step program. I hadn't given OA a thought in years but I found myself saying, "What about OA?" This time I met people who not only accepted me but could care about someone as worthless as I thought I was.

I was hurting so badly I was willing to do anything — get a sponsor, attend as many meetings as possible, use the telephone, give service. After bingeing for the first two months or so I began to catch hold of the abstinence I have today.

As I grow and change in recovery my abstinence changes. Without any plan on my part, the amount of food I eat keeps getting smaller and smaller. I just can't, and don't want to, eat as much as I used to. I avoid certain things, but I've never had a food plan. That's not my path, although I do sponsor those who use them. For me, a food plan is the same as a diet, and I've lost over 128 pounds so far by not dieting. I can't explain how that could have happened — except my Higher Power doing for me what I could never do for myself.

It hasn't always been a steady loss. There have been times

when I've gained two or three pounds, but I've learned that if I leave it alone and turn it over to my Higher Power, the weight will be taken care of without me trying to fix it.

My life is very different from what it was three years ago. I have a Higher Power and a faith. As I write this, I'm sitting on a pillow. Two weeks ago, I had surgery to remove excess skin. Twenty-five pounds of skin were removed in two operations this summer, and there will be at least one more.

Yesterday I turned forty-one. Thanks to OA, I didn't die at forty. I've been jet-skiing and parasailing, and I'm looking forward to learning to skydive. I'm still about fifty pounds overweight, but my Higher Power will take care of the weight loss if I continue to "suit up and show up." I'm a gratefully recovering compulsive eater — and I know for sure that it works when you work it.

Shreveport, Louisiana

PROGRESS REPORT

When I first came into OA more than thirteen years ago, one of the first things my sponsor asked me to do was to write out a history of my weight gains and losses in order to get a clear picture of the nature of my disease. Now, after so many years in OA, I find it useful to review all the different ways I've tried to work this program.

At my first OA meeting I was given a food plan. Abstinence was clearly defined as following this food plan without exception, and committing my food every day to a sponsor. It was very easy to know when I broke my abstinence: An extra lettuce leaf meant that I had to restart the abstinence count from zero. A lot of things depended on clean abstinence back then, such as the right to be a sponsor, which required twenty-one days of back-to-back abstinence.

It was all made very clear, but nonetheless I could never stay abstinent for more than twelve days in a row. Although learning that I had a disease and was not just weak-willed lightened my load, I still felt like a failure because I could never achieve long-term abstinence. Furthermore I felt like a fraud because I never talked about my problems. But, in spite of it all, I gave service, including sponsoring. But, oh, how I struggled with abstinence.

Then a new spirit entered OA. It became accepted that some members needed to work a spiritual program in order to become abstinent; that abstinence was a result of spiritual progress.

What an enormous relief! I worked very hard on the steps, doing a thorough fourth-step inventory and I really tackled my character defects. I wasn't gaining any weight; in fact I was a little bit thinner. More importantly, I no longer felt guilt nor dishonesty. This was liberating.

I'm grateful for this period in my OA life because it succeeded in eliminating the guilt I was still carrying about my compulsive overeating. But even then long-term abstinence did not appear. Furthermore I stopped dealing with the food altogether. I no longer worried about what I was eating or how. I did more than give up the scale and the measuring cup — I gave up abstinence as a goal.

During this period of time I was diagnosed as an active diabetic who had to stay on a very careful diet in order to prevent long-term complications. The dietitian gave me a food plan to follow, but I didn't: I just couldn't somehow, perhaps because I didn't have the tools to handle food restrictions as a goal. Or perhaps I believed that it would be all right if I just worked my program, came to meetings, did service, and turned the problem over to my Higher Power.

Two years ago my diabetes worsened, and the dreaded complications became evident. My way may have given me emotional and spiritual progress, but my eating habits were killing me. I didn't know what to do.

Finally I confided in a close OA friend, a nurse, and said I needed help. The experts she sent me to all said that I had to change my eating habits. I really tried, but still I felt it would all work out if I just went to a lot of meetings and did a lot of service.

Nothing much changed. My life was out of control, my food was out of control, and I was slowly killing myself—all the while going to five meetings a week and working my program as hard as I could.

Five months ago I had a spiritual awakening of the kind I'd always dreamed about. Sitting in my room feeling that I had to choose between life and death (and an ugly death at that), I chose life.

The meaning of that decision became immediately apparent. It meant I had to declare complete bankruptcy and to surrender totally. In this case surrender clearly meant doing anything and everything I was told to do by my doctor, my dietitian, my sponsor, and the OA literature — everything, without selection, and without exception.

The dietitian told me what to eat and how often, and to follow that plan exactly. It is my abstinence, and it is the most important thing in my life without exception. My doctor tells me what to do and I do it, without complaining. The program tells me that I must be honest and not hide anything, even the smallest issue, and so I'm doing that.

For the first time in more than thirteen years in OA, I am experiencing long-term, continuous abstinence. For the most part the compulsion to overeat has been lifted, and for this I am very grateful.

It is not because I am a diabetic that I can be abstinent — I couldn't be abstinent for years in spite of the fact that I knew what the diabetes was doing to me. I am abstinent today because I have a program that gives priority to abstinence. I take care of the food and the rest just happens.

My program is not the same one I worked thirteen years ago. Now I know that the spiritual and emotional growth I've experienced in OA is part of the entire recovery process. And now there's no guilt associated with less than one 100 percent perfect adherence to a food plan — I just keep trying to make progress.

Israel

Eight

WHAT ABSTINENCE HAS TAUGHT ME

PLUGGED INTO RECOVERY

February 10, 1964, is a date I will never forget. It was my first OA meeting. I was fifty-eight, I weighed around 270 pounds, and I was still searching for the magic diet that would do what no other had.

I stormed out of the meeting because what I was hearing was "an insult to my intelligence."

I went to another meeting the very next night. I identified with the speaker and decided to give it a chance. OA was on probation.

AFTER TWENTY-TWO YEARS OF ABSTINENCE, MY WEIGHING AND MEASURING DAYS ARE A LONG WAY BEHIND ME.

At this second meeting I was introduced to the "gray sheet." I got a scale and a cup as had been suggested, and I was ready for business. I was told that I couldn't trust my judgment, and that it would help if I called my food in to someone every day, making the commitment to eat exactly what was measured out. The result would be nirvana!

After twenty-two years of abstinence, my weighing and measuring days are a long way behind me. Recently I heard someone share that she's been in the program for twenty-one years and still calls in her food. To each her own, is something I've learned through twenty-nine years in the program. I'd like to share some other things recovery has taught me.

- To be gentle with myself. I realize that I'm not bad if I stray, or good if I abstain.
- To give up trying to control anything or anyone outside myself.
- To become increasingly honest and open with at least one other person: my sponsor.
- To accept myself exactly as I am without hiding, distorting, or rejecting any part of myself.
- To forgive myself and others. By blessing those who have harmed me, I find peace instead of resentment.
- To live a joyous, peaceful, fulfilled life, I must engage in a search for my inner strength that I now call God.

- That a Power greater than myself is guiding my life whether I recognize it or not.
- That every step has a principle, and I will be enriched by applying all the steps in my daily life.
- That the promises come true.
- That no one ever starves to death between meals.
- That to be on amicable terms with my family is a God-given gift.
- That every meeting adds to the recovery.
- That I cannot do it alone.
- That half measures avail me nothing.
- That writing is an indispensable method of finding out what's amiss.
- That I can live without fear.

SERENITY INSTEAD OF FEAR

Today I was fired. My supervisor cussed at me and told me to leave. I made it clear in a moderate tone of voice that this behavior was inappropriate and would not be tolerated. I calmly walked out on a job I'd had for nine years. Yet I was neither angry nor filled with remorse. Why? Serenity.

I drove home and explained the situation to my eldest son. We talked about my future plans and the goals I hoped to achieve. I ate my planned meal without wanting to sabotage my abstinence.

> YET I WAS NEITHER ANGRY NOR FILLED WITH REMORSE. WHY? SERENITY.

After lunch I immediately began to research new employers. Then I took my children to a park. My sons fed the ducks and I thanked my Higher Power for the opportunity for change and growth. As a single parent, I was concerned about the imminent future, but I wasn't afraid. I felt proud and grateful for the way I had held my ground and retained a professional demeanor.

After mowing the lawn, going to baseball practice, eating an abstinent dinner, and playing a game of Monopoly, I found my copy of *Lifeline* in the mailbox. A perfect end to one day without fear!

Anonymous

THE IMPORTANCE OF BEING HONEST

"If you want to develop self-esteem, you'll have to engage in estimable behavior — behavior worthy of esteem." That's what my sponsor told me throughout the first six months of my program.

Coming to OA 150 pounds overweight and just out of the hospital following two suicide attempts, I was willing to listen to almost anything. But when my sponsor told me this, I was almost at a loss. I had alienated so many people and done so much harm while I was overeating, I doubted I had much to offer. What could I do that was estimable?

AN EMPLOYER ASKED ME TO DO SOMETHING WHICH WAS A CLEAR VIOLATION OF THE LAW.

Following a lengthy rehabilitation, I was able to return to work for a temporary agency. While on an assignment, an employer asked me to do something which was a clear violation of the law. Since he offered me increased wages, I didn't miss a beat: I gladly accepted the offer. A feeling of misery swept over me. It didn't take much consultation with my Higher Power to understand the cause.

I debated what to do for the rest of the day, and then I explained to my employer that I would be happy to do the work but only in an honest manner. He was caught off guard, as if I'd been the first to turn down his lucrative offer. I was both nervous and excited.

From that day my self-esteem began to grow. My shaky abstinence solidified and has been strong ever since.

We're all given the opportunity to perform estimable acts — sometimes in unexpected ways. I think that means we all have the ability to develop better self-esteem. It's only a decision and an H.P. away.

Winfield, Illinois

HEALING ROOM

I've spent two days waiting outside an intensive care unit as my great-aunt slowly slipped away. Grief has not caused me to overeat and for this I'm grateful to my Higher Power.

Today I'm at home tending to everyday business with the realization that anytime now, my mother will call to tell me of my great-aunt's death. Because of the OA program I can still live this day serenely.

Over the past two days I've caught myself thinking, "It's no surprise you're not bingeing. She's not really that close to you anyway." But I remind myself that, in the past, any situation that was out of my control and affected my family gave me a reason to eat.

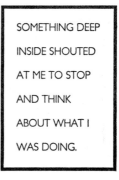

SOMETHING DEEP INSIDE SHOUTED AT ME TO STOP AND THINK ABOUT WHAT I WAS DOING.

The program has given me the gift of abstinence, and today I see how much healing has taken place in my relationships as well.

I've become very close to my mother over the past three years. It wasn't always that way, especially during my high school years. Back then we were about as distant as the earth from the moon. I cut off relations with my family in order to nurture an unhealthy dependence on my boyfriend. The more I tried to secede from my family, the more control my mother tried to exert over me, and there were many unpleasant memories,

Once I got into the program and began to work the steps, I made amends for my actions and laid that part of my past to rest. We still weren't friends, though. Because my husband's family lived in the same town and got together regularly, I unconsciously left mine behind.

Three years ago my life changed. A disabling accident forced me to depend on my mother for housekeeping. But she did more than keep house. She kept me focused on living one day at a time and provided me with love and companionship. She also gave me hope that one day I would recover to the point of being able to live my life more fully.

ONCE I GOT INTO THE PROGRAM AND BEGAN TO WORK THE STEPS, I MADE AMENDS FOR MY ACTIONS AND LAID THAT PART OF MY PAST TO REST.

As my great-aunt began having more and more health problems, I saw how unselfishly my mother cared for her, too. Although I couldn't sit for long, we'd visit her together at the hospital and nursing home. Watching my mother, I saw her ability to set her own life aside when someone else was in need.

Two days ago the nursing home called me and asked for my mother, then apologized for having called the wrong number. I asked what condition my great-aunt was in. They said her blood pressure had dropped so low they'd sent her to the emergency room. I went there immediately.

I'm amazed that I was able to be patient enough to wait. It's another gift of the program. Most of my life I've been overly busy, creating stress when I didn't find enough of it around me. Before OA I ran from anxiety into food and excessive activity.

But today and during the past two days I could be there for my family, especially my mother who would have never asked me to stay but thanked me for coming when I did. I was able to return in a small way some of the love and companionship I've received from her.

I was one of the last two people my great-aunt saw before she lapsed into a coma. I told her which of her sons was out in the waiting room and when the other would be flying in. I was there for her. Before I became abstinent I couldn't have done even that much.

Oh, how healing the program is!

Blair, Nebraska

A BOUQUET FOR ABSTINENCE

About four months ago I'd established a working relationship with a loving Higher Power and the food obsession had been removed. Since then I'd been experiencing the "contented abstinence" so often spoken of in OA. One day last week, however, I got into self-pity so intensely that before I knew what hit me, the obsession was back!

I was at work and not feeling well. I'd planned to go home early to try and get some rest, when all of a sudden the idea hit me: "I'll stop by the nearest store on the way home, get all of my favorite binge foods (yes, all of them!), pile them in front of the TV, and eat—just like old times!" I was actually planning to go through with it. I was tired of feeling bad and desperately wanting a pick-me-up.

> I REMEMBERED HOW GOOD IT FELT TO DO SOMETHING LOVING FOR MYSELF. THOSE FLOWERS SAVED MY PRECIOUS ABSTINENCE.

Something deep inside shouted at me to stop and think about what I was doing. Did I actually want to get back into that old behavior? "Yes!" I shouted back to the voice inside. "I'll just go ahead and get it over with — then it won't bother me anymore," I rationalized. How many times had I used that line before?

Before I left work I decided to listen to my inner voice for a minute. What was I feeling? What did I really need? "Hmm," I said to myself, "I'm feeling down because I'm sick, and I'm bored from sitting around all week. What I really want is to have some fun!" My old way of having fun was to binge and watch TV. But that didn't work anymore. What else could I do?

I thought for a while about what I might enjoy doing. I love to read, so I decided to go home and curl up with a good book I'd bought a while back and hadn't yet had the chance to read. That sounded like fun. Then I remembered what I'd heard my sponsor say several times: "If you're getting into negative behavior, choose to do something positive to counteract it. It's impossible to be both negative and positive towards yourself at the same time."

Then it struck me: I'd go buy myself some flowers. I immediately forgot all about the planned binge and started thinking about what kind of flowers I could treat myself to. I decided to get the flowers, then spend the rest of the afternoon reading my book and enjoying them. I really got excited about the idea—just as I once did about food.

I headed for the nearest florist. To my delight they had an arrangement designed for sending to a person who needs cheering up. It was just what I needed, filled with colorful flowers and festooned with rainbow decorations. It cost a little more than I had planned to spend, but I recalled all the times I'd spent twice that much on food. I was worth it.

When the woman behind the counter said to go ahead and pick out a card and sign it, I thought, "Why not?" I found one with balloons on it, wrote myself a little love note, and put it in the envelope. I didn't tell her the flowers were for me. It felt kind of neat. I thought of all the times I'd bought huge quantities of food at the grocery store and the funny looks and comments I'd gotten from the people behind the counter. This sure felt a lot better than that.

I had a wonderful afternoon reading my book and enjoying my flowers. The best part is that it's been a week and those flowers still look pretty. If I'd binged it would have been over in about fifteen minutes, and I would have been miserable. Each time I looked at my flowers this past week, I remembered how good it felt to do something loving for myself. Those flowers saved my precious abstinence.

Tallahassee, Florida

A LEARNING PROCESS

When I first started OA, the only time I didn't eat was when I absolutely couldn't — like when I was on the production line at work. For the first three months of going to meetings, I listened with inward terror as people talked about three meals a day, and some even talked of weighing and measuring their food.

At about the three-month mark, I got a sponsor and somehow got in the frame of mind to try eating just three times a day with a couple of snacks in-between. To my surprise, it worked. My meals were huge and long-lasting, but for the first time I had a little structure.

During the next couple of years, the quantity as well as the quality of my food changed. I learned more about my body and the medical problems I had that required me to avoid certain foods. The fact that I could avoid those foods most of the time was miraculous to me. My life was changing, too, since OA meetings cut into the time I would normally have spent eating. And the program itself had an impact on me as I identified with others, became more thoughtful about the way I lived, and made some successful attempts to change.

At about the two-and-a-half-year mark, I was eating healthy foods in the right amount most of the time. I saw, however, that I was looking forward to lunch or dinner with the passion of an addict. Even though my food was good, my attitude was as compulsive as ever.

It has just been in the last twelve months, six years into the program, that I have been able to come to the dinner table and say to God, "if you want me to change anything about what I am about to eat, I am willing to do what you want." I still struggle

> OVER THE YEARS THE DEFINITION OF ABSTINENCE THAT I KEPT COMING BACK TO WAS "FREE-DOM FROM COM-PULSIVE EATING."

every day with my food compulsion, but I am happy that many times the struggle can be short-lived and require little effort.

Over the years the definition of abstinence that I kept coming back to was "freedom from compulsive eating." Abstinence is more of a learning process to me than a fixed way of eating. I have learned that I used to see food as a poison like alcohol or drugs. I am coming to appreciate it, just as I am coming to appreciate myself.

I define my relapses as grossly stepping out of bounds of what is normal eating for me. Attending more meetings and the resulting attention to the program always puts me back on track.

Aurora, Colorado

WITHOUT DELAY

Prior to coming into the Overeaters Anonymous Fellowship in 1976, my life was one of total procrastination. As my compulsive overeating progressed, so did my procrastinating. Accomplishing anything at all was a struggle.

My children were eleven and twelve years old when I came into OA. I always had piles of their clothes that needed to be ironed or mended, but I'd end up ironing what was needed the morning of the school day and often bought new clothes to avoid fixing a hem or replacing a button.

I was restless, irritable, and discontented all the time, yet I continually took on additional projects at church and work, never knowing how to say no. If I did say no, I feared I wouldn't be liked. The more projects I took on, the more I procrastinated.

The more I procrastinated, the more frustrated I became. The more frustrated I became, the more I compulsively ate. Always the same cycle that I couldn't get off.

Then I came into OA. It didn't take me long to become abstinent, and hand-in-hand with my abstinence came the beginning of my recovery from procrastination. I remember clearly when a button popped off a sweater and I sewed it on immediately. I felt so good about that simple task. I also began to say no when asked to do things that I didn't have time for. I had come to realize that my self-worth wasn't based on doing whatever was asked of me.

As I learn to take care of myself, to say no when appropriate, to put "first things first," and to work the twelve steps, my procrastination and my other character defects are slowly disappearing. It is difficult to put into words the gratitude I feel towards my Higher Power and the Fellowship of Overeaters Anonymous. The best way I know today is to share it with whomever God puts in my path.

Elyria, Ohio

BLESSINGS GALORE

Recently I had an opportunity to serve as the leader for an OA meeting I attend. To prepare for my pitch, I wrote a list of the many blessings I have come to enjoy in my two years of recovery in OA. The list is long and growing daily. Here are some of my favorites:

- I have learned that in all situations and circumstances, my attitude determines my experiences. I am blessed with the power of choice; an "attitude of gratitude" is the one that serves me best.
- I have a steadily improving relationship with my Higher Power. What was once a fear-filled and unpredictable association is now a loving interaction. I am learning the joys of

prayer through daily meditation and the Serenity Prayer.

- I enjoy unconditional acceptance as an OA member, and, in turn, my acceptance of others both in and out of OA has risen dramatically.
- I have made a commitment to be good to myself, which includes eating well-balanced and abstinent meals, expressing my feelings readily, making time each morning for meditation and prayer, and regularly attending OA meetings. I've redefined my standards for myself, and now aim for progress, not perfection. I feel good about myself!

> I'VE REDEFINED MY STANDARDS FOR MYSELF, AND NOW AIM FOR PROGRESS, NOT PERFECTION. I FEEL GOOD ABOUT MYSELF!

- My relationships with my husband and children are flourishing in the sanity of abstinence.
- I have lost forty pounds and am still losing. For the first time in my life I have hope for staying thin as long as I continue to live the steps and use the tools.
- "Bad" times help me to grow, and they pass in time.
- I've learned it's okay to depend on others. I can't work this program alone. I need my H.P., my sponsor, and my many OA friends who share their love and experiences of recovery.
- Taking life "one day at a time" and turning matters over to H.P. steadily removes fear and worry from my life. I'm learning to distinguish between those things that are my responsibility and those that are not.
- Blessed with priceless serenity I have truly experienced freedom from the bondage of eating compulsively. Each day I become more aware of the plentiful blessings in my life.

OA has helped me to enjoy the adventure of living. Thanks to this twelve-step program, my life is memorable, not miserable.

Kansas

THE TWELVE STEPS

1. We admitted we were powerless over food—that our lives had become unmanageable.

2. Came to believe that a Power greater than ourselves could restore us to sanity.

3. Made a decision to turn our will and our lives over to the care of God *as we understood Him*.

4. Made a searching and fearless moral inventory of ourselves.

5. Admitted to God, to ourselves, and to another human being the exact nature of our wrongs.

6. Were entirely ready to have God remove all these defects of character.

7. Humbly asked Him to remove our shortcomings.

8. Made a list of all persons we had harmed, and became willing to make amends to them all.

9. Made direct amends to such people wherever possible, except when to do so would injure them or others.

10. Continued to take personal inventory and when we were wrong, promptly admitted it.

11. Sought through prayer and meditation to improve our conscious contact with God *as we understood Him*, praying only for knowledge of His will for us and the power to carry that out.

12. Having had a spiritual awakening as the result of these steps, we tried to carry this message to compulsive overeaters and to practice these principles in all our affairs.

Permission to use the Twelve Steps of Alcoholics Anonymous for adaptation granted by AA World Services, Inc.

The Twelve Traditions

1. Our common welfare should come first; personal recovery depends upon OA unity.

2. For our group purpose there is but one ultimate authority—a loving God as He may express Himself in our group conscience. Our leaders are but trusted servants; they do not govern.

3. The only requirement for OA membership is a desire to stop eating compulsively.

4. Each group should be autonomous except in matters affecting other groups or OA as a whole.

5. Each group has but one primary purpose—to carry its message to the compulsive overeater who still suffers.

6. An OA group ought never endorse, finance, or lend the OA name to any related facility or outside enterprise, lest problems of money, property, and prestige divert us from our primary purpose.

7. Every OA group ought to be fully self-supporting, declining outside contributions.

8. Overeaters Anonymous should remain forever nonprofessional, but our service centers may employ special workers.

9. OA, as such, ought never be organized; but we may create service boards or committees directly responsible to those they serve.

10. Overeaters Anonymous has no opinion on outside issues; hence the OA name ought never be drawn into public controversy.

11. Our public relations policy is based on attraction rather than promotion; we need always maintain personal anonymity at the level of press, radio, films, television, and other public media of communication.

12. Anonymity is the spiritual foundation of all these traditions, ever reminding us to place principles before personalities.

Permission to use the Twelve Traditions of Alcoholics Anonymous for adaptation granted by AA World Services, Inc.

For more information on Overeaters Anonymous
or for a copy of OA's literature catalog, write to
the World Service Office, P.O. Box 44020,
Rio Rancho, NM 87174-4020
or find us on the Internet
www.overeatersanonymous.org